FINDING YOUR SUNRISE

Rediscover Life's Beauty Through Adversity

RAVI VASTRAD

Ark House Press
arkhousepress.com

© 2025 Ravi Vastrad

All rights reserved. Australia's copyright laws protect this book. This book may not be copied or reprinted for commercial gain or profit. Short quotations or occasional page copying for personal or group study are encouraged.

Scripture quotations are taken from the HOLY BIBLE, NEW INTERNATIONAL VERSION. Copyright © 1973, 1978, 1984, International Bible Society. Used by permission of Zondervan. All rights reserved. All emphasis within Scripture quotations is the author's own.

Scripture is taken from the New King James Version. Copyright © 1982 by Thomas Nelson, Inc. Used by permission. All rights reserved.

Every effort has been made to ensure the accuracy of the online resources at the time of publication. However, the author and publisher are not responsible for future changes or updates to this online content.

Cover Design By: Good Job Studios |goodjobstudios.com.au
Interior Layout By: Initiate Agency | initiateagency.com

For information on foreign distribution, reach out to us on the internet:
Truth To Nations|truthtonations.com
Or Email: info@truthtonations.com

Cataloguing in Publication Data:
Title: Finding Your Sunrise
ISBN: 9781763880184 (pbk)
Subjects: REL012170   RELIGION / Christian Living / Personal Memoirs

ENDORSEMENTS

I have had the privilege of knowing Ravi for many years, both as a dear friend and as a valued collaborator in various initiatives aimed at helping individuals grow as disciples of Jesus. His focus has been guiding others to recognise and fulfil God's intended purpose for their life. Ravi writes from his heart, drawing from his life experiences. So, his book is not theoretical—it offers practical and powerful wisdom that anyone can apply to become all that God has designed them to become.

Ray Graetz – *Brisbane, Australia (whyamihere.net.au)*

Finding Your Sunrise by Ravi Vastrad is a compelling testimony of God's transformative grace and unfailing love. Ravi's journey from academic success through moments of despair to a life redeemed by faith is relatable and inspiring. His honest reflections on doubt, pride, and the pursuit of truth resonate deeply, while his encounters with God's mercy remind us of the hope found in Christ.

This book is more than a narrative—it's an invitation to rise above life's darkest valleys and experience the healing and freedom that come through a personal relationship with Jesus. Anchored in Malachi 4:2,

Ravi's story testifies to God's faithfulness, encouraging readers to find their own 'sunrise' in His perfect plan.

Pastor Anil Kant - *Founder of Anil Kant Ministries International and Zindagi Forever Church.*

We live in a fallen world, facing many challenges—physical, spiritual, financial, and mental. Yet, as Jesus said, "In this world, you will have tribulations. But take heart! I have overcome the world." God's grace remains sufficient in every difficult situation.

This book, written by my brother-in-law Ravi Vastrad, is a powerful testimony of God's goodness and mercy during one of the most challenging times of his life. It reveals how this experience led him to a profound, personal encounter with Jesus Christ. This is a must-read for anyone facing adversity, offering hope, encouragement, and inspiration. Congratulations, Ravi—may God continue to bless you as you share His love and grace worldwide.

Rev. Dr. Sam Masilamoney – *First United Protestant Church of Hilo, Hawaii, USA*

I have known Ravi and Merlyn for over 30 years and witnessed their journey through the darkness after migrating to Sydney. During that time, Ravi had yet to find faith in Jesus, but through prayer and God's mercy, he experienced a personal 'sunrise.' This book is a powerful reminder of God's unconditional love and grace, inviting readers to experience His transformative power. My prayer is that all who read it will be touched by this truth.

Mary Devadas – *Sydney, Australia*

Finding Your Sunrise tells the story of someone who has embraced the light of the Son, allowing it to shine brightly in his life. For over 20 years, it's been my privilege to know Ravi Vastrad—a man of honesty, integrity, courage, and conviction. May the warmth and challenge of this book stir your heart as you journey through each chapter with Ravi and witness his sunrise.

Wendy Megchelse – *Queensland, Australia*

This past year, Ravi and I met each week to pray and seek God's inspiration together. Through our close friendship, I've observed a man who begins each day in God's presence, from which he always has a joyful word and insight to share. Our most fearful moments can pivot our lives in unexpected directions. For Ravi, these events took him on a journey of transformation from darkness to light, from despair to joy. In FINDING YOUR SUNRISE, you'll discover how this transformation took place and how you can know the same.

Tony O'Hagan – *Queensland, Australia*

Finding Your Sunrise shares Ravi's journey from academic success to a life-altering test of faith. After migrating to Australia, his world was shaken when his wife faced critical surgery while pregnant. In his darkest hour, Ravi reached out to God, seeking hope. Anchored in Malachi 4:2, this story reveals how God's light can pierce the darkest moments, inspiring readers to find their own 'sunrise' through trust in His perfect plan.

As his child, I've always known my dad as a man who fears the Lord, shares the gospel openly, and lives with unwavering faith. My life is a testimony to his perseverance, and we pray that this book inspires you to discover the transformative love and mercy of the living God.

Roshni Harding – *Media Advisor South Australia*

Finding Your Sunrise follows Ravi's transformative journey from traditional Hindu beliefs to a life-changing encounter with Jesus, the Eternal Light. This moment reveals the importance of a personal relationship with Christ, who declared, *"I am the Way, the Truth, and the Life."*

The book inspires truth-seekers to uncover profound truths and experience the power of knowing Jesus personally.

Ps Sam Chidamber – *Queensland, Australia*
Chair - Mission Matters Conference

Ravi and Merlyn Vastrad are dear friends, and I can personally attest to Ravi's integrity, honesty, and genuine, down-to-earth faith. As an obstetrician, I am aware of the life-threatening challenges they faced and the profound wake-up call to faith that followed. Ravi writes with clarity and passion, using vivid metaphors and Spirit-led reflections on the events that shaped his journey. I hope every reader will be inspired to trust in the Saviour he now follows with unwavering fervour.

Dr Harvey Ward – *Gynaecologist, Obstetrician, Australia*

Finding Your Sunrise is a rich exploration of the human experience—what it means to face death, contrasted with the true joy of everlasting life. Ravi Vastrad writes from a deep well of personal experience. His journey with Christ invites us to look inward, helping us see the world around us more clearly. An encouraging story of wisdom and grace that will inspire every generation.

Kendall Gliding – *Journalist | TV Presenter | MC Australia*

Ravi's story of transformation is as powerful as it is relatable. Anyone reading this beautifully written tale will find themselves drawn in, imagining themselves right there beside Ravi, receiving the same insights and revelations, and being challenged to make the most of the possibilities placed before them through God's grace.

Clifford Morgan – *Psychologist and Author, Australia*

In a time of turmoil worldwide, Ravi Vastrad's Finding Your Sunrise provides a clear and refreshing guide to God's truth, goodness, and beauty.

Using Scripture and his personal experiences, Ravi demonstrates how to navigate life's hardships, strife, and challenges by applying our faith to God's Holy Scriptures, especially His promises.

Ravi's many experiences as a child, as a young man, and as a mature family man display clear examples that God is faithful and true to His promises to guard, to guide and to bless believers throughout their lives. Ravi's personal stories consistently testify that God is working in this world and the lives of individuals.

Finding Your Sunrise will assist you in finding and living in the light of "God's sunrise" – the light of the Lord Jesus Christ, the Saviour of the world. I highly recommend this book to any reader who wants to learn more about how to live in the abundant life that God has made available to every individual on this earth.

Dr. Terry Harding – *Brisbane, Australia*

As Ravi's Pastor, I've had the joy and privilege of seeing firsthand Ravi's passion for reaching people for Jesus. His own story of coming alive to faith in Jesus is compelling and moving. *Finding Your Sunrise* reads like a testimony of someone who has allowed the Son to shine deeply into the most personal corners of his life and, in doing so, brings warmth and light to others.

Ravi is a man of honesty, integrity and unwavering conviction. I believe you will be challenged and stirred as you read his story, insights and journey of faith.

Nathan Bean – *Senior Pastor, Nexus Church, Brisbane, Australia*

CONTENTS

Endorsements		iii
Acknowledgements		xiii
Introduction		xv
Chapter 1	A Sunrise in the Shadows of Death	1
Chapter 2	A Sunrise Encounter of the Supernatural	17
Chapter 3	The Genesis of A Sunrise Baby	33
Chapter 4	A Sunrise of Unseen Grace	47
Chapter 5	The Sunrise and the Death of a Karma	60
Chapter 6	Early Childhood of the Sunrise Baby	73
Chapter 7	A Tender Sunrise and Success	89
Chapter 8	An Exodus: A Sunset for A New Sunrise	106
Chapter 9	A Sunrise in the Promised Land	119
Chapter 10	A Sunrise Over Shadows of Sin	134
Chapter 11	The Power of The Sunrise	146
Chapter 12	The Eternal Sunrise	166
Notes and Bibliography		198

Dedicated to my Parents

My Father, Sri. Prof. V. G. Vastrad
My Mother, Smt. L. V. Vastrad

Dedicated to My Family

My father-in-law, Sri. M John
My mother-in-law, Smt. Pushpam John
And to my wife, Merlyn Vastrad

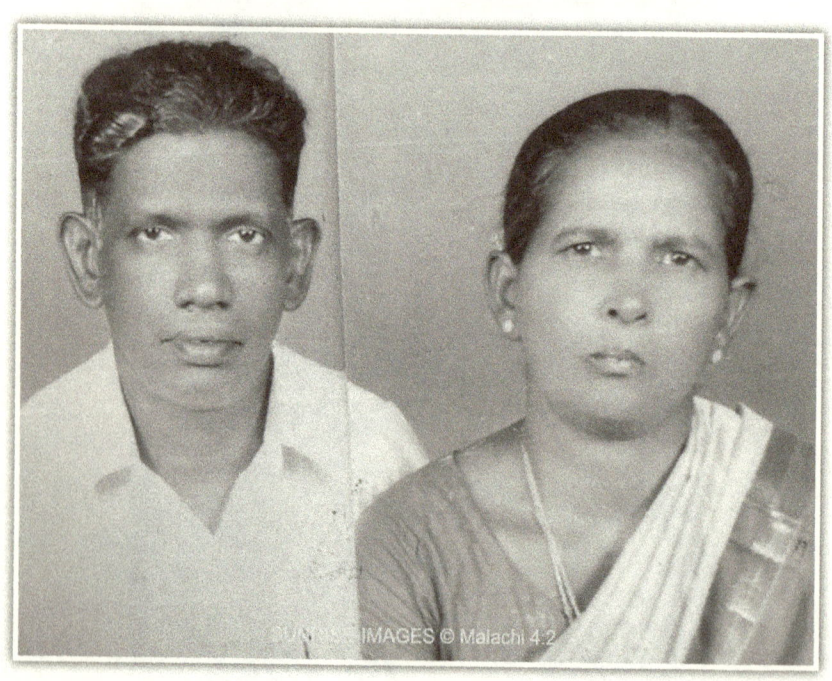

ACKNOWLEDGEMENTS

I am deeply grateful for the unwavering support, love, and prayers that have surrounded me throughout this journey. First and foremost, I extend my heartfelt thanks to my wife, Merlyn, whose constant encouragement and steadfast faith have been a source of strength and inspiration. To my daughter, Roshni, and my son-in-law, Joel, Terry Harding, for your love and prayers, have lifted me in more ways than words can express. Your belief in me has been a profound blessing.

To my church faith family, your companionship on this path of faith has been invaluable. Your prayers, fellowship, and genuine care have sustained me through every step.

Special thanks to Elizabeth Swanson for her meticulous editing, generous support and encouragement, and Ray Graetz for his prayers and incredible insights that enriched this work beyond measure. Your wisdom and kindness have left an indelible mark. And our prayer intercessors Aunty Caryl, Mary and all our faith Family.

I also want to acknowledge my faith family in Sydney and across the globe. Your collective encouragement, prayers, and shared passion for faith have been a continuous source of hope and motivation. Thank you for being part of this journey and for the ways you have contributed to this endeavour.

With all my heart, I am grateful to God for surrounding me with such amazing people who have played significant roles in bringing this work to fruition. May this be a testament to the power of faith, community, and love.

INTRODUCTION

I grew up beneath a tapestry of stars, the clear night sky in India cradling me in its embrace and filling my childhood with wonder. During sweltering summer nights, my family sought refuge from the heat on our rooftop, where the gentle breeze and twinkling stars provided solace in the absence of fans or air conditioning.

Lying there, I would gaze upward, my imagination bursting with questions for my mother:

Who made these stars, Mum?

My little eyes reflected the starlight above, wide with wonder.

How are they formed?

I'd ask breathlessly, as though the answer was a secret the night might reveal.

And how many stars light up the sky?

My voice would trail off in awe, as if counting them was a task we might attempt together.

Little did I know that two decades later, the answers to these questions would emerge from an unexpected source—The Holy Bible. A *divine sunrise* would illuminate my soul, revealing an awe-inspiring creation crafted by the hands of God.

Through the work of the Holy Spirit, I began to comprehend the majesty of creation. The Scriptures came alive, providing clarity and purpose. The simple but profound opening verse of Genesis—*In the beginning, God created the heavens and the earth.* Genesis 1:1 was like a camera shutter capturing an eternal truth. This realisation eclipsed the theories of my formal education, including the "Big Bang theory…," as I grasped the foundational truth of Psalm 33:6:

> *By the word of the Lord the heavens were made, and all their host by the breath of His mouth.*

I exclaimed with exuberant joy, *"Praise The Lord!"*

Raised in a family unfamiliar with God's Word and steeped in cultural traditions, the story of creation was a mystery to me. However, over 27 years ago, during a moment of profound despair, I made a solemn vow: If the God of the Bible can rescue my wife and unborn child, I will seek to know Him personally. That promise marked the beginning of a transformative journey.

Through prayer and dedicated study of the Scriptures, I uncovered a truth that completely transformed my perspective:

- *God is real and He longs for a personal relationship with us.*
- *The Holy Scriptures are a wellspring of hope for all humanity.*
- *Life is not a series of random events but a divine journey—a chance to reflect heaven on earth.*
- *We are fearfully and wonderfully made in the image of our Creator.*

This experience changed everything for me. Suddenly, the world felt new and full of life. The flowers in my garden looked brighter, and even drinking a glass of water felt special. It was as if I was seeing everything

INTRODUCTION

for the first time. I had become a new person, deeply aware of the beauty around me and the goodness of God.

Then I understood the Bible's truth that we need a fresh start to truly know God and have a close relationship with Him. Jesus said, *Very truly I tell you, no one can see the kingdom of God unless they are born again* John 3:3.

Being "born again" means starting a new life with God at the centre. It changes how we see ourselves, helps us understand why we are here, and leads us to our true purpose in life.

Inspired by this revelation, I began sharing the Creation story and teaching others how to conquer anxiety and find peace through the Scriptures. *I will lie down and sleep in peace, for you alone, O Lord, make me dwell in safety.* Psalm 4:8

A wise man of God once advised me that if I didn't document my journey, I would deprive future generations of valuable wisdom and fail to live as an effective witness. His words ignited a passion within me to document my story—not as a personal achievement but as a testimony to the power of God.

This book is the narrative of my pursuit of the Star Maker, the Miracle Worker, and the Creator. Through the Bible, I unearthed life's true purpose—a story of triumph over darkness, life over death, and hope over despair. From the beginning, the Creator's wisdom has brought light and hope to a suffering humanity.

Your Creator knows you intimately and invites you to experience His goodness. Like a jigsaw puzzle, the pieces of life often seem scattered and confusing. Yet, through the Creator's guidance, they come together to reveal a beautiful and fulfilling plan.

I invite you to join me on this journey. I hope that this story will help you **find your new beginning**—your "sunrise"—and break free from struggles that may have affected your family for generations.

As the prophet Isaiah reminds us, **God has incredible power to strengthen us and help us face all of life's challenges.**

> *Look up into the heavens. Who created all the stars? He brings them out like an army, one after another, calling each by its name. Because of His great power and incomparable strength, not even one is missing.* Isaiah 40:26.

The Word of God is the ultimate truth. But truth isn't just an idea—it's a person: **Jesus Christ.** My prayer is that as you take this journey toward your own **"sunrise,"** you will discover the beauty of God's amazing plan and purpose for your life.

This book's 12 chapters take you on a journey of discovery. Each chapter unveils mysteries through the light and love of God's amazing grace. At the end of every chapter, you'll find three interactive life questions designed to help you open up and rediscover life's beauty—even amid the challenges you and your loved ones face.

The Bible is not merely a religious book; it is a divine revelation of our relationship with the Creator of the universe. God is not concerned with man-made religions but desires a personal connection with each of us. This story is not about conversion to a particular belief system or group—it is an invitation to experience a personal *sunrise*, a new beginning, and step into the purpose-built life God designed for you.

This story is about a genuine relationship with God, not religion, which is the essence of eternal life. John 17:3 states: *Now this is eternal life: that they know you, the only true God, and Jesus Christ, whom you have sent.*

Revelation 3:20 States: *Here I am! I stand at the door and knock. If anyone hears my voice and opens the door, I will come in and eat with that person, and they with me.*

INTRODUCTION

God invites you into a personal relationship with Him.

The story of God's redemption and reconciliation is truly extraordinary, and **I encourage you to dive in and examine the credibility of this narrative for yourself.**

CHAPTER 1

A Sunrise in the Shadows of Death

*Even though I walk through the valley of the shadow of death,
I will fear no evil, for You are with me.* Psalm. 23:4

The Abyss and the Miracle: A Journey of Faith, Fear, and Sunshine

Life, with its unpredictable twists and turns, has a way of bringing us to our knees. For many, the moments of deepest despair are where the most profound transformations occur. My journey bridges the abyss of death, the torrents of destruction, and the miraculous grace that emerged from the shadows of the darkest days of my life. As I have reflected on my life and viewed it through God's living word, I marvel at the works of my Creator.

The Beginning of the Descent

It was supposed to be a time of joy, celebrating new beginnings. My wife and I had just migrated to a new country, Australia, filled with hope and dreams of a bright, prosperous future. We were expecting our first child, a beacon of light in our lives. We were ready to embrace the unknown, excited by the promise of what lay ahead. Little did we know that our faith, our strength, and our very lives would soon be put to the ultimate test.

The news hit us like a thunderbolt—a cruel twist of fate that shook us to our very core. My pregnant wife was diagnosed with a severe spinal condition, one that required an urgent and complex surgical procedure: a laminectomy. The doctors, speaking with clinical detachment, laid out the grim reality before us, leaving us grappling with the weight of the situation.

A **laminectomy** is a surgery that involves the removal of a portion of the vertebral bone called the lamina, which covers the spinal cord. It is often performed to relieve pressure on the spinal cord or nerves.

This procedure was necessary to remove an Arteriovenous malformation (AVM) located around the spinal cord.

During pregnancy, the growing baby caused increasing pressure from an abnormal tangle of blood vessels (AVM) near the spine, specifically around the T6 and T7 vertebrae. This severe compression of the spinal cord disrupted nerve signals, resulting in progressive paralysis from the waist down.

The surgery was both complex and dangerous, made even more challenging by the advanced pregnancy. Although the doctors expressed cautious optimism about the outcome, they warned us of the potential need for an emergency C-section to save the baby. Then came the most chilling words of all—they were prepared for the possibility of losing both lives.

Due to the high risks involved in saving the lives of my wife and our 29-week-old baby, the hospital staff asked me to sign a consent form. It was, without a doubt, the most daunting signature I have ever had to make. In that moment of fear and uncertainty, an emergency surgery was quickly arranged at this highly reputed hospital. None of the doctors had ever attempted such a complex surgery in their practice before.

When the neurologist shared the MRI scan report and explained the complexity of the situation, it felt as though the ground beneath me had vanished, leaving me to plunge into an abyss—a bottomless pit of fear, helplessness, and despair. It was as if the cords of death had tightened around me, dragging me into a suffocating darkness. The torrents of ruin and the overwhelming streams of hopelessness engulfed me, and I could see no escape. At that moment, I had never felt so alone, so utterly terrified.

The Desperate Cry

My wife, however, was made of a steadfast soul. Despite the fear and uncertainty, her faith in Jesus (Yeshua) surged to the forefront. She was a woman of deep belief, and she knew that in this moment of crisis, she had to lean on her faith more than ever before. She urged me to call upon our family, friends, and church community to intercede on our behalf, to pray for a miracle, and to seek the mercy of God.

The Misunderstood Concept of Karma

Growing up, karma was ever-present in my life. I often heard it in conversations with family and friends. Yet, despite how common it was, karma always felt vague and misunderstood. It was portrayed as some cosmic ledger, balancing the good and the bad in life, promising that every action—whether ours or our ancestors'—would eventually bring reward or punishment. The idea of "generational karma" loomed large, as if the misdeeds of those before me could control my destiny. It felt heavy and threatening, as though unseen forces determined the course of my life, beyond my ability to change.

The Weight of Generational Karma

During some of my darkest moments, believing in karma offered no peace. Instead of bringing comfort, it felt like a cruel reminder that my hardships and misfortunes were the unavoidable consequences of past wrongs. It filled me with fear rather than hope—fear that I was bound to repay debts I never incurred. Many saw karma as a law of balance and justice, but to me, it seemed more like a burden too heavy to bear.

A Skeptic's Perspective on Faith and Karma

I was not a man of faith at that time. I believed only in what I could see, touch, and reason through. I thought life was about effort and logic, not unseen spiritual forces. Prayers felt empty, and miracles seemed like fairy tales to comfort those desperate for answers. I had believed that we carved our destiny with hard work and rational thinking, not through faith in the divine.

But then, something changed. As I stood beside my wife in a moment of deep uncertainty, I saw in her eyes both fear and unwavering faith. She believed in something greater—something I couldn't measure or explain. In that moment, my heart longed for hope, even as my rational mind resisted. I felt torn between the scepticism I had clung to and the possibility that there was more to life than I understood. It was a stirring I couldn't ignore.

I later discovered that what my heart longed for was not found in karma or fate but in the grace and truth of Jesus Christ. The Bible revealed a different reality—one where we are not trapped in an endless cycle of repayment for past wrongs but are offered forgiveness, new life, and freedom through faith in Him.

The Turning Point - A Glimpse of Faith

That moment became a turning point. I didn't suddenly embrace faith or understand everything overnight, but something inside me began to shift. I started to question the certainty of my beliefs. Was there more to life than logic and reason could explain? Could it be that life wasn't just about retribution or balancing cosmic scales, but about something deeper—something that points to purpose, hope, and transformation?

A Journey Toward Understanding

For much of my life, I believed in karma—the idea that every action brings a reaction and that we reap the consequences of our choices. I thought karma was something to fear, but over time, I came to see it as incomplete. While it teaches that our actions matter, it doesn't offer real hope, forgiveness, or freedom from the cycle of consequences.

The Bible, however, revealed something far greater. It's not about balancing good and bad deeds; it's about God's grace. Scripture teaches that while we do reap what we sow (Galatians 6:7), God offers mercy that breaks the cycle of condemnation. Through Jesus Christ, we are offered forgiveness and a new life—not because we deserve it, but because of His love.

As Ephesians 2:8-9 declares, *For it is by grace you have been saved, through faith—and this is not from yourselves, it is the gift of God—not by works, so that no one can boast.* We don't earn God's favour through good deeds or religious effort; salvation is a gift to those who believe in Jesus.

Trusting God's Bigger Plan

I didn't find all the answers right away. I'm still on the journey. But I've come to understand that hope isn't found in having everything figured out. True hope comes from trusting that God has a bigger plan—even when we don't fully understand it. Life isn't about fear or striving to earn divine favour. It's about trusting in God's love and resting in His grace.

Every choice we make matters. But what gives life true purpose is the love of God, which redeems and restores us through Jesus Christ. Life isn't meant to punish us; it's meant to lead us to the One who offers forgiveness, freedom, and eternal life.

Why Karma Falls Short

In Chapter 5, I explain why I believe karma is a false and deceptive human belief. It denies God's grace and the finished work of Jesus Christ, trapping people in an endless cycle of striving, guilt, fear, and spiritual deception. The good news is that Jesus broke that cycle. At the Cross, He made a way for all who believe to receive freedom, forgiveness, and new life—once and for all.

The Miracle of Life

The hours leading up to the surgery felt like an eternity. Each tick of the clock echoed in my mind, amplifying the fear that gripped my heart. But during this fear, something extraordinary happened—a sense of peace began to wash over me. It was as if my desperate cry had been heard, and a response, gentle yet powerful, was making its way back to me.

The surgery began, and with it, the agonising wait. My wife was in the hands of the surgeons, but **I believed, for the first time in my life, that she was also in the hands of something much greater—God's hands.** As we waited, the prayers of our loved ones filled the air, creating a tapestry of faith that covered us like a warm blanket on the coldest of nights.

Then came the news—the surgery was successful. Both my wife and our unborn child were safe. The relief was overwhelming, the joy indescribable. The torrents of destruction that had threatened to drown us had been held at bay by a power I had only just begun to understand. The cords of death that had encircled us had been cut, and life had prevailed.

But our journey did not end there. The recovery was slow and fraught with challenges and setbacks. There were moments of doubt, moments when fear tried to creep back in. Yet, there was also a new strength—a strength born of faith, of the knowledge that we were not alone in this struggle. We had been touched by the miraculous, and it had left an indelible mark on our souls.

Years later, I read a miraculous medical report from the surgeon: The doctors decided to operate urgently to relieve pressure on her spinal cord while taking extra precautions to protect the baby. She (my wife) was positioned on her left side, and special equipment was used to support all vital circulations and monitoring during the procedure.

During surgery, the medical team discovered an abnormal tangle of enlarged, high-pressure blood vessels near the spine, which began bleeding immediately. The surgeons carefully sealed these vessels to stop the bleeding.

The main cause of progressive paralysis was a cluster of tangled blood vessels near the T6 and T7 areas. Despite losing about a litre of blood, her blood pressure remained stable. The team successfully addressed the critical issues while safeguarding both mother and baby.

My Second Brush with Death

The following day, still reeling from the events of the surgery, I experienced another brush with death. Exhausted from the sleepless night and the emotional toll, I got into my car to fax an urgent visa application for my wife's mother. So she could come from India and be a great comfort and help us. My mind was foggy, and I was completely exhausted. As I drove, the tiredness and anxiety weighed heavily on me. The roads were slick and wet from the rain. I could feel my eyelids growing heavy, my grip on the steering wheel loosening. And then, in a terrifying instant, I lost control of the car.

Time seemed to stretch and blur as my vehicle careened off the road. The barrier raced toward me in a terrifying rush, and instinctively, I squeezed my eyes shut in fear. But as panic gripped me, I found my voice, and I cried out, "Oh God, save me!" These words came out of my heart in an instant. The car spun wildly, beyond my control, skidding across the road as the screeching of tyres against asphalt pierced the air. The violent jolt coursed through my body, each impact a shockwave of terror. Yet, when my car finally came to a halt, a surreal stillness fell over me. I was alive, shaken, but miraculously unharmed. Once again, death had knocked at my door, and once again, I had been spared. Then, I knew it was yet another miracle. My life had been granted a new lease by the Lord. Here I stand today, a living witness to this truth. My life was spared for this very moment—to testify to the power of prayer.

As I stood beside my car, my heart pounding in my chest, I knew that something had changed within me. I had faced death twice in 24 hours, and both times, I had been delivered from its grasp. There was no denying it any longer—faith in Jesus was becoming real, and it worked for the humble and the poor in spirit. It was not just something my wife believed in; it was something I had now begun to experience firsthand.

At The Cross Street

To my amazement, I saw that my car had somehow come to a stop on the other side of the road. But what left me truly stunned was how perfectly it was parked, right next to the curb, as if guided by an unseen hand. And it was facing the opposite direction.

Years later, as I was reflecting on this incredible experience, I felt a strong urge to visit the exact place where my life had been spared. When

I arrived, I looked up at the street sign and was quietly amazed—it was called "Cross Street."

Isn't that remarkable? It reminded me of the **cross of Jesus Christ**, where the greatest exchange took place: **death for life, darkness for light**. It was at the cross that Jesus rescued us, giving us hope and a new beginning.

Then, I wondered in my mind, asking myself, 'Why was my car facing the opposite direction?' Then, I understood the power of repentance. To repent of pride and sin means to make a 180-degree turn from our lifestyle.

The Bible reveals a profound truth: at the cross, Jesus took my place, dying the death I deserved, and in doing so, He spared my life. It was a divine exchange—His sacrifice for my salvation. This extraordinary moment was not the end but the beginning of a journey filled with more divine exchanges. With each step, I experienced His grace, mercy, and unfathomable love.

Now, as I reflect on this journey, I can confidently testify that even in the darkest valleys, when death seems near, you can call upon the Lord. His promises are true, and His Word is unwavering.

No matter how deep the despair or how great the danger is, when you trust in Him, He will save you. This truth is not just a teaching—it is a living reality I have witnessed firsthand.

To me, the cross is not just a symbol of sacrifice; it is a profound reminder of the eternal hope we have in Christ. It marks the place where death was defeated and new life was given. For every believer, this divine exchange is available—a powerful testament to God's love and faithfulness, even in life's most challenging moments.

A New Beginning...

In the days and weeks that followed, I began to reflect on all that had happened. The fear, the despair, and my desperate cry for help had brought me to a place I never thought I would be. A place of faith, of hope, of understanding that there is a power greater than us that is always watching, always listening, always ready to step in when we have reached the end of our strength.

I became a witness to this truth, not just for myself but for others. My story, our story, became a testament to the power of faith and prayer, a beacon of hope for those who find themselves in the darkest of places. We had walked through the valley of the shadow of death, and we had emerged on the other side, not unscathed but stronger, wiser, and with a renewed sense of purpose.

The Journey Continues...

Today, as I reflect on holding our healthy child in my arms and see the smile on my wife's face, I am reminded of the journey we have taken. It was not an easy road, but it brought us closer together and closer to the truth that there is a divine presence in our lives, guiding us, protecting us, and offering us hope even in the most hopeless of situations.

The cords of death no longer surround me. The torrents of destruction have receded, replaced by streams of grace and mercy. I have learned that in our moments of deepest despair, when we feel like the ground is giving way beneath us, there is a hand that reaches out to pull us back from the brink—a hand that belongs to the One who knows us, even when we do not yet know Him.

This marked the beginning of my new sunrise—a fresh season in my life. It was at this moment that I realised how many times I had narrowly escaped death. My parents often reminded me of the close encounters I had with it, stories that I will share in this book. But this isn't just a tale of survival; it's a story of profound transformation. It's about discovering faith when I thought I had none and experiencing the power of prayer when least expected.

Looking back, I see now that every brush with death wasn't just a coincidence. Each one was a step toward something bigger, something more meaningful. It's a reminder that no matter how dark the night gets, the dawn will eventually break. And when it does, it brings with it the light of hope and redemption.

I am no longer the person I once was. I am forever changed—forever grateful. This journey has filled me with a deep commitment to share my story with others, hoping they, too, can find strength in their darkest moments. Because sometimes, when we cry out from the depths of our pain and fear, we discover a power we didn't know we had—something miraculous that can only be unlocked with an open heart.

Ancient Truth Is Still Alive

I encountered the powerful expressions of King David as he faced death. It is powerfully expressed in this Scripture:

> *I called to the Lord, who is worthy of praise,*
> *and I have been saved from my enemies.*
> *The cords of death entangled me;*
> *The torrents of destruction overwhelmed me.*

The cords of the grave coiled around me;
The snares of death confronted me.
In my distress, I called to the Lord;
I cried to my God for help.
From his temple, he heard my voice;
my cry came before him, into his ears.
Psalm 18:3-6

David's words resonate deeply with my own experiences. Like him, I have faced moments when death felt like it had wrapped its cords around me, and the overwhelming forces of destruction threatened to take everything. Yet, in those times of distress, I called upon the Lord, and just as He did for David, He heard my cry.

It was a profound realisation that this ancient truth still holds today. The same God who rescued David is the one who saves us now. When we are entangled in fear and danger and overwhelmed by life's storms, we can trust that God hears our cries and is attentive to our needs. Just as David experienced deliverance, so have I—and I stand as a living witness to the enduring power of God's salvation.

As we reflect on our life's valleys, we must also remember the call of Scripture to endure and be transformed. The Holy Bible, particularly in Romans 12:2, tells us to *repent and renew our minds, to not be conformed to the patterns of this world, but to seek God's will—a path that leads to hope, purpose, and a life driven by faith.*

This kind of mind renewal allows us to see beyond the immediate darkness of our trials and glimpse the greater purpose that God is unfolding in our lives.

Conclusion: Renew Your Mind

I will never forget my journey through the valley of the shadow of death. It was a time marked by deep fear and uncertainty, yet it became a powerful and life-changing encounter with God. It all began when my wife faced a life-threatening surgery during her pregnancy. Overwhelmed with fear and questions, I cried out to God—and He answered. By His grace and mercy, both my wife and our unborn child were miraculously saved.

Not long after, I survived a near-fatal car accident. Once again, I experienced God's divine protection. At that moment, I knew my life had been spared for a greater purpose—perhaps for such a time as this (Esther 4:14).

Through these experiences, I came to understand the reality of God's presence and the power of prayer. He is not distant or silent. He is near to all who call on Him in truth (Psalm 145:18). He hears, He saves, and He walks with us through every trial.

Now, I invite you to reflect on your journey. Are you walking through trials, facing despair, or carrying burdens too heavy to bear?

The Bible calls us to renew our minds (Romans 12:2). This renewal begins when we turn away from old ways of thinking, surrender our lives to God, and allow His truth to transform us. No matter how dark the valley is, God's light can break through. His love leads us to healing, renewal, and a life of faith.

Repentance—turning away from sin—and transformation through Jesus Christ is the only path to lasting hope and strength. He is the Good Shepherd, and He promises to lead us even through our darkest moments (Psalm 23:4). He offers peace, hope, and deliverance to those who place their trust in Him.

Let my story be a reminder: no matter how deep the valley, there is always a way forward when we place our faith in God's sovereign plan. Renew your mind. Embrace His purpose for your life. Let your faith carry you through to the other side—where hope rises and a new beginning awaits.

This first chapter marks the beginning of a miraculous journey. In the chapters that follow, you'll witness the supernatural hand of God guiding my path. Along the way, you'll also have the opportunity to discover your true identity through the light of His amazing grace.

"Every day a million miracles begiin at sunrise."

Eric Jerome Dickey

Living the Message: Practical Questions

1. What difficult moments have you faced that made you question everything? How did you feel God's presence during those times?

   _____
   _____
   _____

2. How can you use Scripture to change your perspective during tough situations and trust God's plan for your life?

   _____
   _____
   _____

3. Reflecting on your struggles, how might you trust God's plan more fully and allow your faith to guide you toward healing and hope? Additionally, how can you shift your mindset from blaming your challenges on bad karma to taking full responsibility for your actions?

   _____
   _____
   _____

CHAPTER 2

A Sunrise Encounter of the Supernatural

For nothing will be impossible with God. Luke 1:37

Some time ago, I experienced a moment that changed my life forever. It was a time when I was simply going about my daily routine, yet I had no idea that what I was about to encounter would completely reshape my worldview, ignite a spiritual awakening, and connect me deeply with my Creator. This is the story of that supernatural vision and the series of events that led to it.

Even though I had walked through the valley of the shadow of death, my faith in Jesus was not unwavering. I longed for a deeper understanding of faith and answers about my life's purpose. I had many profound questions and believed only one person could provide the answers I sought.

Invitation to Seek the Divine

In 1998, I received an invitation to attend a small local church congregation in Western Sydney. I didn't anticipate anything unusual or extraordinary, just a normal Sunday gathering. The church was small, and the community was welcoming, but what struck me was the message delivered that day. The preacher spoke with conviction, challenging us to reflect on our lives and ask ourselves a difficult question: *Is there anything in my life or my home that does not honour God?*

This question lingered in my mind long after the service had ended. I had been a person of some faith, but I had never taken the time to reflect deeply on how my lifestyle might be inconsistent with the teachings I professed to follow. The message penetrated my heart, stirring within me a desire to seek God more seriously. I needed to know if there were things in my life that displeased Him, so I turned to God in prayer, asking for His help in revealing anything that stood between me and a deeper connection with Him.

A Spiritual Cleansing

Soon after that prayer, I felt convinced to clean up my life, starting with my home. As I looked around, I noticed things that seemed innocuous but now felt like barriers to my spiritual journey. One by one, I began removing these obstacles. Alcoholic drinks were the first to go. I realised they had become an unnecessary presence in my home, subtly detracting from my life. With each bottle discarded, I felt a weight lift off my spirit.

Next, I turned my attention to my entertainment choices. I had a collection of Bollywood music tapes that I enjoyed listening to, but as I reflected on them, I realised much of the content didn't align with a godly lifestyle. Without hesitation, I tossed them into the waste bin, feeling a growing sense of freedom with each step. While many Indian movies have inspired me, others have distorted my perspective on life.

However, as I sorted through my collection, I came across one unique cassette tape. It was a Bible teaching tape, though I didn't know much about the speaker at the time. Something within me prompted me to listen to it, but I didn't do so immediately. It wasn't until later that I decided to play it in my car while driving—a decision that would change my life forever.

The Awakening Begins

As I drove, I inserted the cassette tape into the player, unsure of what to expect. The opening sentence of the message instantly captured my attention. It wasn't like anything I had heard before—it was as though the speaker was speaking directly to my soul. The message began with an observation that was simple yet profound:

> *"In a human head, there are seven natural openings—two eyes, two ears, two nostrils, and one mouth…and nobody wants two mouths…we have enough trouble with one mouth…"*

I didn't know it at the time, but this was no ordinary Bible teaching. The speaker was Derek Prince, a renowned Bible teacher. The message centred on the power of the tongue immediately resonated with me. Derek Prince spoke about how the mouth, the tongue in particular, is a tool of great power—both for good and for harm. As he spoke, I felt an intense stirring in my spirit. His words carried wisdom beyond human experience, piercing straight into my heart. I will never forget that moment because it felt as though I was standing on the threshold of something monumental.

A Whisper in the Spirit

As the speaker began recounting the creation story from the book of Genesis, describing how God created man in His image and likeness with the ability to think, speak, and communicate constructively, something extraordinary happened. In the middle of his teaching, I heard a gentle whisper in my spirit. The voice was clear and calm, yet undeniable: *"That is the truth. Receive it".*

For a moment, time seemed to stand still. I had never experienced anything like this before. The whisper was not external but internal—it resonated within me, directly to my soul. In my heart, I responded, "Yes,

Lord, I receive this truth into my heart". Immediately, a gentle stream of peace began to flow through me, calming my mind and heart in a way I had never known. The message continued, and the speaker quoted a verse from the Scripture: *By the word of the Lord, the heavens were made, and by His breath, all the starry hosts.* Once again, I heard the same whisper, "That is the truth, receive it". This time, the impact was even greater. I responded again, "Yes, Lord, I receive this truth," and at that very moment, something incredible happened.

The Vision Unfolds

Suddenly, it was as though my spirit came alive in a way I had never experienced before. My subconscious mind, my inner being, was awakened. Words from Genesis 1:1 flashed through my mind: *In the beginning, God created the heavens and the earth.* Almost immediately after, the words of John 1:1 came to mind: *In the beginning was the Word, and the Word was with God, and the Word was God.* These verses, combined with the teaching I had just heard, converged in my spirit and pointed me to Psalm 33:6: *By the word of the Lord, the heavens were made, their starry host by the breath of his mouth.*

It was at this moment that the supernatural vision began. In my spirit, I saw a person in the form of brilliant, radiant light. He was indescribably glorious, and as He opened His mouth, stars flew out, forming galaxies in the vastness of space. The sun, moon, and even our tiny solar system came into being as He spoke. It was as if I were witnessing the creation of the universe firsthand.

There are no human words sufficient to fully describe the majesty and power of this experience. As I watched, I trembled with fearsome joy and overwhelming peace. The awe I felt was indescribable. I knew at that moment that I was in the presence of the Creator, the One who breathed the stars into existence. I felt utterly unworthy to witness such a sight, and a deep sense of reverence filled me.

For many years, my parents, teachers, and school tried to explain where life came from, but I still did not understand. Then, one verse changed everything for me: Hebrews 11:3, *By faith, we understand that the universe was formed at God's command so that what is seen was not made out of what was visible.* The Big Bang Theory I learned in school no longer made sense when compared to this powerful truth. Hallelujah!

This truth set me free from confusion and darkness. It has become the story of God's great **'Big Breath'**—showing His incredible power and glory. Consider verses from Colossians 1:16 state that everything was created through Him (Yeshua). Also refer to: Revelation 4:11, Isaiah 45:18, and Nehemiah 9:6.

A Revelation of Grace

As I marvelled at the awesome vision, I remembered the words of Isaiah 6:5: *Woe to me! I am ruined! For I am a man of unclean lips, and my eyes have seen the King, the Lord Almighty.* Like Isaiah, I felt unclean and unworthy. Shame and guilt began to creep into my heart, but just as quickly as they arrived, the gentle whisper returned: *Ravi, you have been washed and cleansed by the blood of Jesus, the Lamb of God.*

Instantly, the shame and guilt that had weighed me down were lifted. It was as though chains of religion, pride, and tradition that had bound me for generations were broken in an instant. I felt an overwhelming sense of joy and freedom, a liberation of my spirit that I had never known before.

With this amazing revelation, I could not help but **praise Yeshua** with all my heart. But a question stirred within me—how did our ancestors miss this living truth and the glory of the one true God? Why did they wander like sheep without a good shepherd, unaware of His compassion and grace?

Yet, even as these questions arose, my joy remained overwhelming. Deep within, I knew that one day, God would reveal the answers to me in His perfect time.

Matthew 9:36 states – *When He saw the crowds, He had compassion on them, because they were harassed and helpless, like sheep without a shepherd.* Jesus Himself grieved over those who wandered without knowing God's truth, just as I wonder about my ancestors.

But words Jeremiah 29:13 assured me – *You will seek me and find me when you seek me with all your heart.* This powerful promise reassures you that as you seek answers, God **will** reveal them in His divine timing.

A New Creation: Viewing the World Through New Eyes

Immediately after my vivid supernatural encounter, I felt as though a veil had been lifted from my eyes. It was as if I had brand-new eyesight, a completely fresh perspective on the world around me. At that time, I didn't fully understand what was happening to me. All I knew was that something profound had shifted within me. I wasn't just seeing the physical world differently—my entire perception of life had changed.

One day, as I was reflecting on these changes, I came across the scripture from 2 Corinthians 5:17:

> *Therefore, if anyone is in Christ, he is a new creation; old things have passed away; behold, all things have become new.*

Suddenly, the word lit up my soul like a brilliant sunrise, revealing a profound truth: I am a new creation!

That verse encapsulated my experience, revealing that being a new creation in Christ wasn't merely about faith—it meant embracing an entirely transformed perspective on the world.

I will never forget the morning that changed everything. It's etched in my memory as if it happened just yesterday. The sun was just beginning to rise, painting the sky with soft hues of gold and pink. I took my coffee, stepped into our garden, and was immediately captivated by what I saw.

My wife and I had poured years of care into cultivating this haven, filled with fragrant roses of every shade—deep reds, gentle pinks, and luminous yellows. But that morning, the garden seemed different—alive in a way I had never experienced before.

The roses were in full bloom, their colours so vivid they seemed to glow, and their fragrance filled the air like a symphony of aromas. As I stood there in awe, something extraordinary happened. It was as if the flowers were speaking, gently inviting me to step closer, to marvel at their beauty, and to pause long enough to truly take it all in.

At that moment, I felt an overwhelming sense of peace and gratitude wash over me, a reminder that even in life's darkest seasons, there is a *sunrise* of hope and beauty waiting to be noticed. It wasn't just a garden—it was a message, a gentle whisper from God, reminding me that life, no matter how challenging, still holds moments of joy and wonder if we have the heart to see them.

An Encounter with Creation

I walked closer to the roses, drawn by their scent and appearance. As I bent down to inhale the fragrance, I was overwhelmed by their sweetness. I gently touched the petals, marvelling at their softness. At that moment, once again I felt a deep sense of awe for God's creation. Without thinking, I began to speak to the flowers:

> *Now I know why you are so beautiful...the One who made you is the great Creator... He also created me—fearfully and wonderfully!*

It was as if for the first time, I truly understood the beauty and intricacy of creation. The flowers weren't just plants anymore; they reflected the Creator's brilliance. I praised God for His craftsmanship, for creating something so delicate and yet so full of life. The moment was surreal, but it was also incredibly real. It felt as though I was encountering God in the simplest of things—a flower, a fragrance, a touch. My heart overflowed with gratitude.

Being born again brings us into a living faith and transforms our understanding of ourselves in three profound ways:

1. You cannot truly know yourself until you are spiritually alive.
2. Without the Spirit of God, your true identity and potential remain hidden. *This is a great tragedy.*

3. Being born again by the Spirit of the Living God reveals your deepest and truest self-worth.

This spiritual rebirth is the key to discovering both God and the unique purpose He has designed for your life.

> *Far from disproving the existence of God, astronomers may be finding more circumstantial evidence that God exists.*
>
> Robert Jastrow

Seeing the Ordinary as Extraordinary

Later that day, I went into the house and picked up a glass of water to drink. But before I took a sip, I paused. I stared at the water in my hand, realising that this was not just water—it was a miracle. This clear, tasteless liquid was designed by God to quench my physical thirst, sustain my body, and give me life. How had I gone through life never appreciating something so fundamental? For years, I had taken things like water for granted, treating them as ordinary, routine aspects of daily life.

But that day, everything seemed extraordinary. I was filled with wonder at the thought that even the most basic elements of life were gifts from our loving Creator. I realised that I had never truly thanked or praised God for the things I had always assumed would be there—flowers, water, the air I breathed. It was all part of His beautiful design, and yet, I had overlooked it for so long. As a **new creation in Christ**, my spirit was awakened to **connect deeply** with the beauty and power of **God's glorious creation**.

A New Perspective on Relationships

This newfound awareness didn't just change how I viewed nature; it also transformed my relationships. Suddenly, the people in my life mattered more deeply. Every interaction had a new sense of meaning and importance. I found myself caring more about how I treated others, how I spoke to them, and how I could serve them. I began to see the image of God in everyone around me, and this awareness gave me a profound sense of love and responsibility toward others.

My relationship with my wife grew stronger as I became more attuned to the ways I could honour her and show her love. My friendships deepened as I sought to be more present, more understanding, and more compassionate. Even my interactions with strangers became opportunities to reflect the love of Christ.

I started greeting people with a simple "Hi," but it was no longer just a casual word. It had grown into something much deeper and more meaningful. Every time I said it, I consciously acknowledged the profound truth that each person I encountered was created in the image of God. It wasn't merely about saying hello—it was about recognising their inherent worth as someone divinely crafted by the Creator Himself. And that is the power of a transformed mind.

Each greeting carried a silent message of respect and honour, a reminder to myself that the person in front of me, no matter who they were or where they came from, reflected God's image. This realisation changed the way I interacted with people. Whether it was a stranger on the street, a coworker, or a family member, my simple "Hi" became a way to express a deeper connection, recognising that they, like me, were fearfully and wonderfully made.

This shift in my perspective made even the smallest encounters feel sacred. It was no longer about just passing by people without thought; each interaction became an opportunity to acknowledge the divine spark within them. I realised that by greeting others with this mindset, I was not only expressing kindness but also honouring God's creation in a simple yet profound way.

Then I realised that the **Indian greeting, Namaste,** carries a similar gesture. **Namaste** is a traditional greeting that means **"I bow to you,"** derived from the Sanskrit words **"namah"** (bow) and **"te"** (to you). It is typically performed with palms pressed together near the chest with a slight bow of the head. This simple yet profound gesture symbolises **respect, humility, and the recognition of the divine presence within each person.**

Sharing the Joy of the Lord

In the days that followed, I carried this newfound joy with me everywhere I went. The joy of the Lord had truly become my strength, and I couldn't help but share it with others. I remember carrying my Bible to work the following week, eager to talk about my experience with my coworkers. Whenever the opportunity arose, I would share the story of my encounter with the Creator, explaining how it had changed my life and given me a new understanding of the world.

People could see the difference in me—there was peace and joy that I hadn't had before. I wasn't just sharing words; I was sharing the truth of what had happened to me, and it was evident in the way I lived and spoke. This wasn't something I had learned from a book or a sermon; it was a living, breathing reality in my life.

A New Reverence for the Word of God

As I continued to grow in my faith, I found that my relationship with the Bible had also changed. I began to read the Word of God with a newfound reverence and love. It wasn't just a book of teachings and stories anymore—it was the living Word, full of truth and life. Every passage spoke to me in a personal way, and I approached each reading with a sense of anticipation, knowing that God had something to reveal to me through His Word.

In the weeks that followed, I sought the help of Scripture to fully understand and interpret my experience. I realised that what I had witnessed wasn't just a vision of creation—it was a revelation of God's immense power and love. The vision was a reminder that we are not merely physical beings; we are spiritual beings created in God's image, with the ability to think, speak, and connect with the Divine. This realisation deepened my relationship with God and gave me a greater sense of purpose in life.

Fundamental Flaws in the Theory of Evolution

During one of my teaching assignments, a student asked me to give an example of why many people question the theory of evolution. Without much thought, I picked up my wristwatch and posed a simple question to the class:

Can this watch evolve over millions of years into what it is today? Or if we dismantle its parts and melt them down, could it ever reassemble itself into a perfectly working watch—on its own?

The classroom fell silent. No one was quite sure how to respond.

Then I explained that our human bodies—and all of life—are far more complex than a watch. If a simple object like a watch requires a designer to make it and put it together, how much more does life require an **Intelligent Designer and Creator?**

In my study and research, I found many credible scientists and scholars who challenge the claims and assumptions behind the theory of evolution. While evolution is widely accepted in the scientific community and often taught as fact, there are serious and thoughtful critiques that cannot be ignored.

Here are **three major challenges** that many have raised against the theory of evolution:

1. *Challenges in Explaining Complexity:* Some scientists argue that random mutations and natural selection alone cannot account for complex, "irreducibly complex" structures that fail to function if even one part is missing.
2. *Debates Over Mechanisms:* Researchers question whether current evolutionary theory fully explains life's complexity, suggesting it may require significant revisions.
3. *Lack of Observable Evidence:* Critics highlight the absence of direct observation of evolution in progress, citing clear gaps between distinct "kinds" of plants and animals.

Conclusion: A Life Transformed

That supernatural encounter gave life to my spirit in a way that words alone cannot fully describe. It was an amazing and intimate experience with the One who loves me deeply, and it completely changed the way I saw the world. I became a new creation in Christ, not just in name but in how I viewed every aspect of life. Nature, relationships, and even the most ordinary things like water were now filled with meaning and wonder.

Looking back on that experience, I can see that it was a turning point in my spiritual journey. It awakened in me a deep sense of purpose and a desire to live in a closer relationship with my Creator. To this day, I carry the memory of that encounter with me, and it continues to inspire and guide me as I walk in the newness of life that I found in Christ.

I now invite you to pause and reflect on your own life: Are there areas where you feel distant from God?

Have you ever considered that He desires to draw near to you, just as He did with me?

Every moment of our lives offers an opportunity to experience the profound presence of the One who created you, loves you, and longs to reveal Himself to you.

Remember, the theory of evolution faces three major critiques: It struggles to explain "irreducibly complex" structures that cannot function without all parts (*Discovery Institute*). Researchers question its mechanisms, suggesting the theory may need significant revisions (*The Guardian*). Critics also point to a lack of observable evidence, noting gaps between distinct kinds of life forms (*ICR*).

Take a moment to seek Him, ask Him to make Himself known to you in a fresh and personal way. You may be on the brink of a life-changing encounter, one that will awaken your spirit and bring you closer to God than you've ever imagined. Just as my experience was transformative, yours can be, too, by letting God open your eyes to new perspectives, deeper relationships, and a more profound connection with your Creator. The journey begins with a single step, and that step is drawing near to Him, ready to experience His love, grace, and truth in your own life. A step closer to your new sunrise!

> *He gives strength to the weary and increases the power of the weak.* Isaiah 40:29

Living the Message: Practical Questions

1. How can you begin to see the everyday moments of your life, like nature, relationships, or even simple tasks, as opportunities to experience God's presence and wonder?

   _____
   _____
   _____

2. Are there areas in your life where you feel disconnected or distant from God, and what steps can you take today to invite Him into those areas?

   _____
   _____
   _____

3. Have you ever paused to ask God to reveal Himself to you in a personal and transformative way? If not, what might be holding you back from taking that step of faith?

   _____
   _____
   _____

CHAPTER 3

The Genesis of A Sunrise Baby

Every child comes with the message that God is not yet discouraged of man. Rabindranath Tagore.

Do you know...?

That You Are Known Before You Were Born...!

Before I formed you in the womb, I knew you; before you were born, I set you apart.

Jeremiah 1:5

The Miracle of Birth: A Divine Introduction

As I grew up, my parents frequently reminded me of the significance of the day and hour I entered this world. They spoke of it not just as a fact but as a cherished memory filled with meaning and symbolism.

Over the years, their stories helped me understand how deeply they valued that moment. In this chapter, I've taken the time to reflect and recount those details, piecing together the events surrounding my birth as they lovingly shared them with me.

This is my attempt to capture that special moment just as they remembered it. I have gained deeper insights into their story through the lenses of God's word and Spirit. I choose to honour my parents as I recount the story of my birth.

Congratulations, Professor!

The midwife exclaimed, her voice bright with joy.

She beamed as she handed my father his newborn son despite the exhaustion of a long winter night. It was a moment of pure celebration—the gift of new life.

Later in my life, I was reminded of this wonderful word, *Behold, children are a heritage from the LORD, the fruit of the womb a reward.* Psalm 127:3

My grandmother joined in the joy, asking my father, "Today is Sunday, and this baby is born at sunrise. He's a sunrise baby! And your seventh child. What will you name him?"

With a thoughtful smile, my father—a professor and gifted orator—spoke. "Let's name him 'Ravi'. It means 'the sun,' a reminder of this special sunrise and the light he brings into our lives".

What I couldn't comprehend then, I've reflected on over the years. My name, Ravi, came to symbolise far more than a mere connection to the time of day. It marked the presence of divine light in our family—a light that would grow and shine in ways none of us could yet see.

A Father's Legacy: The Symbolism of Forty

When I entered the world, my father was forty—an age steeped in spiritual significance. In the Bible, forty represents a season of preparation, trial and growth. As I reflect on my father's journey and its intertwining with mine, I recognise a divine pattern.

Just as Moses' life unfolded in three stages of forty years, my father, too, had two seasons of forty. First as a professor, then as a man who departed this world at eighty, entering his eternal home. His life embodied resilience and wisdom, and I trust that one day, we will be reunited in heaven.

The Sacred Number Forty: A Period of Transformation

The number forty echoes through Scripture, marking moments of profound change. Moses spent forty days on Mount Sinai, receiving the Ten Commandments. The Israelites wandered for forty years in the wilderness before entering the Promised Land. Noah endured forty days of rain in the flood, and Jesus fasted for forty days in the desert. Each season of the forty trials was a preparation for something greater—a divine purpose unfolding through time.

In my own life, this number resonates as I reflect on my father's journey and my spiritual growth. It reminds me that God uses time—forty days, forty years—to shape us for a higher calling.

The Command to Honour: A Source of Blessing

> *Honour your father and your mother so that you may live long in the land the Lord your God is giving you.*
> Exodus 20:12

This commandment, uniquely tied to a promise, has shaped my life. Honouring my parents wasn't merely an act of obedience; it was a path to blessing and a key to understanding the depth of God's love. My father, despite losing both his parents at a young age, chose a life of faith, resilience, and service, becoming a beacon of hope to many.

His life taught me that honouring those who came before us is more than respect—it's an acknowledgement of their sacrifices and an embrace of the values they passed down. My father lived with grace, and in honouring him, I found strength and direction in my own life. His legacy was a seed planted, and through my actions, I continue to water it, letting it flourish into something lasting and good.

A Mother's Strength: Triumph Over Trials

Like my father, my mother's journey was marked by resilience. Having lost her father and fleeing her hometown, she became a teacher at a young age, raising seven children and guiding twelve grandchildren. Her strength, forged through hardship, became a testament to God's grace. Together, my parents embodied the kind of faith that not only survives adversity but transforms it into a source of strength for the generations to come.

Before they passed, both of my parents reconciled their lives with God, a final act of grace for which I am deeply grateful.

The Sunrise: A Daily Metaphor for Life

The sunrise has always held special meaning for me. It's a symbol of renewal, of life beginning again with the breaking of dawn. Each sunrise tells a story of endurance, resilience, and the inevitability of light returning after darkness.

Just as the sun rises without hesitation, life continues, no matter our struggles. The world keeps turning, offering new opportunities for hope and growth. Every time I witness a sunrise, I am reminded that no matter how dark the night is, the light always returns, illuminating a new path forward.

Finding Renewal in Every Sunrise

The sunrise, for me, is more than a natural event. It's a reflection of the human spirit. Just as the sky brightens, so do we evolve and grow, moving from moments of darkness into light. There are challenges in life, but they are always followed by the opportunity for a fresh start.

In each sunrise, I see a reminder of the hope that resides within us. We are constantly becoming, like the sun's light breaking through the horizon, bringing warmth and clarity to the world. To live fully is to rise each day, no matter the challenges, and embrace the light with hope and gratitude.

Under the Stars: Childhood Wonder

As a child, I often slept under the vast expanse of stars during the warm nights of the Indian summer. Night after night, I would lie there, captivated by the endless heavens above, my heart brimming with wonder and curiosity. My mother, with her gentle wisdom, patiently answered my endless stream of questions about the stars. Her words not only deepened my fascination but also stirred in me a profound awe for the Creator who had masterfully adorned the night sky. Little did I know, those starry nights held a divine message—a glimpse of His infinite love, a love I would come to encounter in a life-changing way years later.

Those starry nights were a constant reminder that the same God who made the stars was also writing a story in my life. Every moment, whether a brilliant sunrise or a silent night under the stars, spoke of His divine presence and love.

A Life of Purpose: Called to Be a Bearer of Light

> *You are the light of the world. A city on a hill cannot be hidden.* Matthew 5:14

My name, Ravi, means 'sun', and it fits the special calling God has for my life. Just as the sun rises each day, spreading light and warmth, I have learned that I am meant to bring light too—not just any light, but the eternal light of the Gospel. This truth has become clear to me slowly, like the sunrise, filling my life with understanding as I follow the purpose God has given me.

As a child, I was affectionately called by my parents "Sunrise Baby", born at the break of dawn, bringing new light into their lives. But as I've grown, I've come to understand that my role extends far beyond that special moment of my birth. My life is meant to reflect a much greater light—the light of Christ. He calls all of us to be "the light of the world," to shine in the darkness, not hidden, but radiant like a city on a hill, visible to all.

The Unfolding of a Divine Calling

From a young age, I felt a sense of significance surrounding my life, though I couldn't always pinpoint it. My parents often spoke about the timing of my birth with reverence, as if it held a deeper meaning. As I matured, I began to grasp that this wasn't merely about the day or hour I was born—it was about the calling that was woven into my very being, even before I took my first breath.

Jeremiah 1:5 states: *Before I formed you in the womb, I knew you. Before you were born, I set you apart.*

This truth resonates deeply with me. I now see that God had a plan for me long before I arrived, and the meaning behind my name was not a coincidence. Just as the sun was created to illuminate the earth, I was born to shine the light of Christ into my family, my community, and beyond. God's purpose for me, like the sunrise, has been unfolding over time—gradually at first, then growing brighter as I've leaned into my calling.

A Life of Purpose: Shining Light in Darkness

The sun does not question its purpose; it simply rises, day after day, fulfilling its role in the grand design of creation. In the same way, I am learning to embrace my purpose without hesitation. God has called me to be a light-bearer, a witness to His love and grace. This calling is not one I chose; it was placed on my life by the One who created me, who knew me before I was formed.

Jesus' words in the Sermon on the Mount—"You are the light of the world"—reveal not just a role but a responsibility. To be the light of the world is to live in a way that reflects the love of God to those around me, to stand firm in my faith like a city on a hill, visible and unwavering in the face of darkness. My life, like a candle in a dark room or the sun rising in the morning sky, is meant to dispel shadows, bring warmth, and offer hope.

I have realised that this light I carry is not mine alone—it reflects the greater light of Christ. Just as the moon reflects the sun's light in the night sky, so too am I called to reflect the light of God's truth and love in the world. Every interaction, every story I tell, every action I take is an opportunity to let that light shine, to share the Gospel, and to guide others toward the source of all light—Jesus Himself.

A City on a Hill: Living a Life That Cannot Be Hidden

The metaphor of a city on a hill speaks to the kind of life God calls us to live—one that is bold, visible, and unwavering. A city on a hilltop, glowing in the night, cannot be hidden. Its light serves as a beacon, a point of reference for those lost in the dark. I believe that my name, Ravi, meaning 'sun,' is more than just a label—it's a calling to live out this truth. My life, like that city on a hill, is meant to stand as a testimony of God's goodness, a guiding light for those who need direction, hope, or truth.

But this calling also comes with challenges. There are times when shining light amid darkness is difficult. Darkness seeks to overwhelm, to hide, and to distort the truth. Yet, it is precisely in those moments that light is most needed. The sun doesn't shy away from the night; it rises boldly every morning, no matter how long the darkness has lasted. In the same way, I am learning to rise, day after day, embracing the role of a light-bearer, even when the path ahead seems uncertain.

A Composer of Story: Sharing God's Love Story

In Arabic and Persian, the name 'Ravi' translates to 'composer' or 'storyteller'. I've come to see this as an essential part of my identity as well. God has called me not only to be a light but also to be a storyteller—a composer of His love and grace. My life itself is a story, one that reflects His greater narrative of redemption, hope, and reconciliation. Through my words, my actions, and the way I live, I am writing chapters in the love story.

Now, I believe that the Gospel is, at its heart, a story—a story of light entering a world of darkness, of hope being restored, and of love conquering all. By sharing my story, I am also sharing God's heart for humanity. Whether through conversations with family, acts of kindness to strangers, or simply living with integrity and faith, I am part of that greater narrative. Each day is a new page in this unfolding story, and I am called to make every word and every action count.

The Light of the World: Reflection of God's Glory

Ultimately, the light I bear is the reflection of my Creator. Jesus, the true light of the world, shines through me and through all who are called by His name. My purpose is to reflect that light, to shine in such a way that others are drawn not to me but to Him. It's a calling that fills me with both responsibility and joy, knowing that my life, though small, can have an eternal impact when it shines with His love.

As I continue to walk this path, I do so with the understanding that God has set me apart for this very reason. He knew me before I was formed, and He appointed me to be a bearer of light. My name, Ravi, is not just a reflection of the sun but of the Son—Jesus Christ, who has called me to shine His light in the world. Just as a city on a hill cannot be hidden, neither can the light He has placed within me. With each new day, I rise with the sun, ready to share that light and to compose the next chapter in the story He is writing through my life.

The Song of Creation: Seeing God in Every Sunrise

Whenever I reflect on my life and the beauty of creation, I am reminded of Phil Wickham's song:

> *You're Beautiful:*
> *I see Your face in every sunrise,*
> *The colours of the morning are inside Your eyes.*
> *The world awakens in the light of the day,*
> *I look up to the sky and say, You're beautiful…*

Each sunrise, every star, is a reflection of God's beauty and love. My life and the lives of my parents are part of that magnificent story. We are each called to be a light, a reflection of His grace in a world that desperately needs it.

As I continue my journey, I carry with me the lessons of resilience, honour, and faith that my parents lived out so beautifully. And with each new dawn, I am reminded that the story isn't over yet—the sun will rise again, and with it, a new chapter begins.

Conclusion

Born at sunrise on a Sunday, my parents named me Ravi, meaning sun, a reflection of light and joy. Their stories of my birth emphasised God's hand in my life, and over time, I came to understand the profound meaning behind my name. My father, a professor and a man of wisdom, was forty when I was born, a number symbolic of transformation in Scripture. His life and legacy, filled with resilience and faith, taught me the importance of honouring those who came before us. My mother's strength through adversity inspired generations of our family, demonstrating the beauty of faith in action.

The sunrise has become a metaphor for my life, symbolising renewal, hope, and divine purpose. It reminds me that no matter how dark life's challenges become, light always returns, bringing opportunities for growth and transformation. My journey of faith has shown me that I am called to be a bearer of light, reflecting Christ's love and truth into the world. Like a city on a hill or the rising sun, my life is meant to shine, offering warmth and guidance to others.

As a storyteller, I see my life as part of God's greater narrative—a story of redemption, love, and purpose. Each day is a new chapter in this divine composition. The name Ravi, which also means storyteller, reminds me of my role to share the Gospel and inspire others to embrace their calling as light-bearers. My life's purpose is to reflect the light of Jesus Christ, illuminating the path for others and drawing them toward God's eternal hope and love.

God Himself is called "Abba."

I grew up calling my father "Abba", while most people in our neighbourhood addressed their fathers as "Appa." Somehow, our family had been influenced to use "Abba" as a term for our dad. This seemingly small difference fascinated me, but it became even more profound when I later encountered the Bible and discovered that **God Himself is called "Abba."**

Romans 8:15 declares:

> *For you did not receive the spirit of slavery to fall back into fear, but you have received the Spirit of adoption as sons, by whom we cry, 'Abba! Father!'*

I was amazed to realise that this word, rooted in Aramaic and Persian traditions, had made its way into South Indian culture. Historically, the Kannada language, especially in regions like North Karnataka, absorbed words from Persian and Urdu due to centuries of cultural exchanges. This linguistic integration reflects the deep connections between language, identity, and faith.

But more than just a historical curiosity, **the Bible reveals a life-changing truth**—when we receive salvation through Jesus Christ, we are no longer strangers, but **adopted as children of God.** Now, we can boldly call Him **"Abba, Our Father"** (Galatians 4:6).

It is incredible to think that the very word I used for my earthly father is the same intimate name given to our Heavenly Father—**the One who loves, adopts, and redeems us through Jesus Christ.**

> *Every sunrise is an invitation for us to arise and brighten someone's day.*
>
> Richelle E. Goodrich.

Living the Message: Practical Questions

1. In what ways can you use your unique story to guide and encourage others toward God's love and truth?
   _____
   _____
   _____

2. What legacy of faith or resilience from your family inspires you to live with purpose and hope?
   _____
   _____
   _____

3. How can you reflect God's light in your daily life, especially during challenging times?
   _____
   _____
   _____

CHAPTER 4

A Sunrise of Unseen Grace

Born in the Shadow of War: Legacy of My Parents

> *Children are a heritage from the Lord, offspring a reward from Him. Like arrows in the hands of a warrior are children born in one's youth. Blessed is the man whose quiver is full of them.* Psalm 127:3-5

In 1924, the world was still grappling with the devastation left by World War I—a time when nations were broken and countless families shattered. Amidst this turbulence, my father was born as the only child of his parents. His birth, while meant to symbolise hope and a brighter future, was soon overshadowed by a series of trials that would shape his life.

Tragedy struck early when my grandfather passed away while my father was still a baby. For my grandmother, the loss was immeasurable, but the burden of raising a child alone in a world that had little compassion for widows added to her grief. Despite the overwhelming challenges, she stood resilient despite adversity, determined to provide for her son.

A Remarkable Woman of Strength and Love

My grandmother was an extraordinary woman who became everything to my father—his teacher, protector, and friend. At a time when women were often underestimated, she defied societal expectations, raising my father with love, resilience, and faith. She became his world, guiding light and strength, providing a foundation to shape his future.

Just as my father began to find his way in life, tragedy struck again. My grandmother, his entire world, passed away, leaving him an orphan at a tender age. The grief and isolation he felt were unimaginable. Young and vulnerable, he was now completely alone, with a void left by the loss of his only anchor.

Guided by an Unseen Hand

Despite the overwhelming grief and adversity, my father refused to give in to despair. Though he felt utterly alone, there was an unseen force guiding him. God, his unseen Father, watched over him and carried him through his darkest moments. Though my father may not have realised it at the time, he was never truly abandoned.

My father's life became a powerful testament to the resilience of the human spirit. Refusing to be defined by the hardships he endured, he used his experiences as fuel for his determination. He poured himself into his studies, driven by a desire to rise above his circumstances and honour the memory of his parents.

A Legacy of Perseverance and Wisdom

Through sheer determination and resilience, my father excelled in his education and went on to become a respected professor. He was not only a man of intellect but also a man of immense character. He taught his students not just academic subjects but also valuable life lessons about overcoming adversity and the power of perseverance. His legacy is one of strength, honour, and the relentless pursuit of a brighter future.

Honouring My Parents

In the Bible, God commands us to *Honour your father and mother, so that you may live long in the land the Lord your God is giving you.* Exodus 20:12

This directive is not just a command but a promise of blessings, longevity, and goodness for those who follow it. As I reflect on the lives of my parents, I realise how deeply they embodied values of perseverance, generosity, and faith, making it a privilege to honour them.

My Father's Journey: Overcoming Hardships

My father's life was a testament to resilience. Despite the challenges and hardships he faced during his childhood, he never wavered in his pursuit of education. God gave him the strength and wisdom to pursue his passion for teaching, beginning as a high school teacher and rising to become a respected professor. His work extended beyond the classroom, leaving a lasting impact on students and colleagues alike. In honouring my father, I recognise that he was fulfilling the role God placed before him—to teach, inspire, and shape future generations.

Spreading the National Language

As my father's calling grew, so did his influence. He became deeply involved in promoting the national language, travelling across South India and sharing knowledge through radio broadcasts. His teachings were filled with joy, practical life lessons, and humour—qualities that made learning accessible and meaningful to so many. His ability to connect with people was a gift from God, and he used it to bless others. By honouring my father's efforts, I acknowledge the purpose God had for him in spreading wisdom and knowledge throughout the land.

Honouring the Legacy: Being Remembered as the Children of Professor Sir

One of the greatest blessings in my life is being recognised as the child of Prof. Sir. The Bible teaches that *A good name is more desirable than great riches.* Proverbs 22:1, and my father's name is held in high esteem by our community. His influence as an educator and a compassionate mentor earned him the respect and admiration of many. By honouring his name, I am also fulfilling the scriptural call to uphold and respect the legacy of my parents.

Reflecting God's Compassion: Helping the Disadvantaged

My father's life mirrored God's command to care for the disadvantaged. He extended his heart and his resources to help students who faced immense challenges, believing in their potential when others might not have. His kindness and willingness to uplift those in need were rooted in the biblical principle of loving one's neighbour as oneself (Mark 12:31). By honouring his legacy, I acknowledge the way he lived out God's love in practical ways, making a difference in the lives of countless students.

Inspired to Excel: My Father's Influence on My Journey

> As the Bible teaches, *Train up a child in the way he should go, and when he is old, he will not depart from it.* Proverbs 22:6.

My father's influence shaped not only his students but also my own life. Teachers who had been inspired by him took a special interest in my success, offering guidance and encouragement that helped me excel academically. This support reflects the blessings of honouring one's parents—God's hand was evident in the doors that opened for me because of my father's good name and reputation.

The Power of Honour

By honouring my parents, I am fulfilling God's command, and in doing so, I am blessed. Their lives of faith, perseverance, and compassion continue to inspire me, and I am grateful to God for the example they have set. Through their legacy, I am reminded that honouring one's parents is not just an obligation but a path to living a long and good life, just as God has promised.

A Father's Journey

As the years passed, my father married and became the father of seven children. To us, he was more than just a father—he was our hero. He provided us with everything he had never known: a stable home, unconditional love, and a deep sense of security. Despite the hardships he had endured, or perhaps because of them, he was an incredibly loving and devoted father. He instilled in us the values his mother had imparted to him: hard work, integrity, compassion, and faith.

But there was one thing my father did not yet know, something that had been with him all along but that he had not fully recognised; the guiding hand of the realisation of God. Throughout his life, from the loss of his parents to the struggles of his early years, God had been there, guiding him, protecting him, and leading him towards his true purpose.

It was not until later in life that my father came to this profound realisation. After years of striving, struggling, and searching for meaning, he finally recognised the presence of the unseen Father who had been with him every step of the way. It was a moment of revelation, a moment of clarity that brought everything into focus. My father, who had accomplished so much on his own, realised that he had never been truly alone.

A Life Transformed: Power of True Surrender to God

The realisation of God's presence in his life was transformative. My father, who had always been strong and self-reliant, understood that true strength comes from surrendering to something greater than oneself. He surrendered his life to Jesus, embracing the faith that had been quietly sustaining him all those years. It was as if a weight had been lifted from his shoulders, as if he had finally found the missing piece of his life's puzzle.

When I became a witness to God's power and shared my testimony with my father, something incredible happened—it transformed him in ways I never expected. For years, my father had lived a life of self-reliance, strong in his convictions and determined to navigate life on his terms. He believed in doing things the 'right way' but had always viewed faith as more of a cultural or religious tradition, something to observe but not necessarily something that held personal significance.

But when I told him about my encounter with God, something stirred within him. He realised that God was not after empty religious rituals or outward appearances—He desired a genuine, personal relationship. This revelation shifted something deep in my father's heart. It was not about checking off boxes or adhering to tradition anymore; it was about connecting with the Creator on an intimate level, about truly knowing Him.

Independence to Surrender: Finding True Peace

The change was almost immediate. My father, once so steadfast in his independence, came to understand that true strength is not found in holding onto control but in surrendering to something greater than yourself. In that moment, he surrendered his life to Jesus, embracing the faith that had been quietly calling him all those years. It was a profound shift—a man who had spent his life relying on his abilities now placed his trust in God's hands.

As he surrendered, I could see the weight lifting from his shoulders, as though he had finally released a burden he had been carrying for decades. It was as if he had discovered the missing piece of his life's puzzle. For the first time, he knew what it meant to experience true peace—peace that comes not from external circumstances but from the assurance that he was held in the hands of a loving and powerful God.

This transformation did not just change his outlook; it changed his entire way of being. The man who had once found security in his strength now found peace in his dependence on Christ. He became more compassionate, more patient, and more open to the world around him. It was as if the hardness in his heart had melted away, replaced by the softening love of God.

The transformation was a beautiful reminder that no matter how strong or self-reliant we think we are, we all need a Saviour. My father's journey showed me that sometimes the greatest strength lies in letting go—letting go of pride, of control, and of the illusion that we can do it all on our own. And in doing so, we discover a power far greater than we could ever imagine. My mother also experienced God's mercy and forgiveness and put her faith in Jesus.

In their later years, as my parents faced the challenges of aging and health issues, they found a profound sense of peace. Their faith in the living God offered them a fresh perspective on both life and death. From that moment, their lives took on a new dimension. My father's faith became the foundation upon which he built every aspect of his existence. It shaped every decision, every action, and every relationship.

The Power of Letting Go: Transformed by Grace

He was no longer defined solely by his roles as a professor, father, or husband. He became a man of deep faith, a servant of the unseen Father who had been quietly guiding him through life's storms. His identity was now rooted in something far greater than earthly titles—he was a man of God, living with a purpose far beyond this world. Faith did not just sustain him; it transformed him, infusing every corner of his life with new meaning and direction.

His faith was not just something he professed; it was something he lived. It was evident in the way he treated others, in the way he loved us, his children, and in the way he approached life's challenges. He became a beacon of hope, a source of inspiration not just for his family but for everyone who knew him.

My father's story is not just a story of survival; it is a story of grace. It is a story of how God can take the most broken and battered among us and use them for His glory. It is a story of how, even when we feel utterly alone, we are never truly abandoned. God is always there, even when we cannot see Him, even when we do not yet know Him.

A Legacy of Faith, Strength: Enduring Testament

As I reflect on my father's life, I am filled with awe and gratitude. His journey was not an easy one, but it was a journey of profound significance. Through every trial and tribulation, he emerged stronger, wiser, and more compassionate. His life is a testament to the power of faith, to the strength that comes from surrendering to God's will, and to the incredible things that can happen when we finally recognise the presence of the unseen Father in our lives.

My father's legacy lives on in the lives of his children and grandchildren. We are the beneficiaries of his strength, his wisdom, and his faith. And though he is no longer with us, his legacy continues to guide us, just as the unseen Father guided him. His story is a reminder that no matter how dark the night, the dawn will always come. No matter how heavy the burden is, God is there to carry it with us. And no matter how lost we may feel, we are never truly alone.

In the end, my father's life was not just a story of hardship and loss; it was a story of redemption, of love, and of grace. It was a story that continues to inspire, uplift, and remind us of the incredible power of an unseen Father who is always by our side.

Isaiah 40:29-31 teaches that *God grants strength to the exhausted and empowers the weak. Even the young grow tired and stumble, but those who place their hope in the Lord will have their strength renewed. They will rise like eagles, run without tiring, and walk without fainting.* My father's endurance through life's hardships is a testament to the strength God gave him, sustaining him just as He promised in his younger years.

Conclusion

My father's life exemplified resilience, faith, and transformation. Overcoming the hardships of his childhood, he pursued his passion for education, becoming a respected professor and mentor. He travelled to South India, promoting the national language, sharing knowledge with joy and humour, and touching countless lives. His kindness, rooted in God's command to love one's neighbour, extended to students facing immense challenges, offering them hope and opportunity.

For years, my father relied on his strength, viewing faith as a tradition rather than a personal connection. However, when I shared my testimony, something shifted. He realised that God desires a genuine relationship, not empty rituals. This revelation led him to surrender his life to Jesus, finding peace and freedom in God's grace. No longer defined by roles or achievements, my father became a man of genuine faith, living with a purpose rooted in God's will.

His transformation was profound—he grew more compassionate, patient, and hopeful. As he faced aging and health challenges, his faith offered him peace and a new perspective on life and death. Together with my mother, who also embraced God's mercy, they experienced the fullness of God's love in their later years.

My father's legacy is one of grace and redemption. His life taught us the power of surrender, the strength found in faith, and the hope that comes from trusting God. His story reminds us that even in life's darkest moments, God is present, guiding us toward His purpose. As Isaiah 40:29-31 declares, *Those who place their hope in the Lord will renew their strength, rise like eagles,* and endure life's trials.

My father's journey continues to inspire me to honour his legacy by living with faith, perseverance, and compassion.

Living the Message: Practical Questions

1. Are there areas in your life where you are relying on your strength instead of surrendering to God?
   _____
   _____
   _____

2. How can you honour the legacy of faith and perseverance in your family or community?
   _____
   _____
   _____

3. What steps can you take today to deepen your relationship with God and experience His transformative grace?
   _____
   _____
   _____

CHAPTER 5

The Sunrise and the Death of a Karma

Do not be deceived: God cannot be mocked. A man reaps what he sows. Galatians 6:7

Do not be deceived

Growing up, my parents often expressed deep emotions whenever misfortune struck our family or friends. They would say, "Ayyyoo... Namma Ketta Karma," which translates to "Oh.... this is our bad karma". This phrase was a way to explain the suffering or difficulties we faced emotionally. It wasn't just my family; it was a common sentiment in our culture. Many people around us believe that tragedies, hardships, and even death result from bad karma, seeing them as the inevitable consequences of past actions.

Like millions of people around the world, I was once completely deceived by the man-made philosophy of karma. In this chapter, I want to share that just as I was set free from this deep and subtle deception, you too can find true freedom and a new beginning through the good news of Yeshua (Jesus). He alone brings light, truth, and the promise of eternal life; and a new sunrise over all our life struggles.

I now understand that karma is a deceptive human belief that denies God's grace and the complete salvation found in Jesus Christ. It keeps people trapped in an endless cycle of striving, guilt, fear, and spiritual deception. To understand why so many remain in this deception, we must look at the root cause of this belief is sin. Because it is sin that blinds hearts and minds, keeping people from the truth and freedom found in Christ.

Life is not based on luck or fate.

What many people call 'luck,' I believe is God's hand at work. I don't see life as random or accidental. Everything happens for a reason, even when we don't fully understand it. The Bible teaches that God is in control of all things, and His plans are good.

Many people believe in **luck**—the idea that life is controlled by chance, random events, or good fortune. They think that if you're lucky, good things happen by accident. If you're unlucky, bad things happen, and it's all beyond anyone's control.

But according to the **Bible**, there's **no such thing as luck**. Life isn't a game of chance. Instead, the Bible teaches that:

- **God is in control** of everything (Proverbs 16:33).
- What happens in life is part of God's **sovereign plan** (Romans 8:28).
- Nothing happens by accident (Psalm 139:16).

When people say, "You're lucky," the Bible would say, "No—God is blessing you," or "God is working things out for a purpose."

For example:

- **Proverbs 16:33 (NKJV)** says *The lot is cast into the lap, but its every decision is from the Lord.* Even what looks like chance (like rolling dice) is under God's control.
- **Romans 8:28 (NKJV)** says, *And we know that all things work together for good to those who love God, to those who are called according to His purpose.*

Exposing the Ancient Roots of Sin

I never truly understood the weight and ancient roots of sin until I experienced my divine sunrise—the moment that transformed me into a man of faith. It happened when I encountered the Creator of the universe Himself. The Bible describes this life-changing encounter as being 'born again'.

We read the words of Jesus in John 3:3, *Most assuredly, I say to you, unless one is born again, he cannot see the kingdom of God.*

A wise man once told me: when your child is covered in filth—dirt, rubbish, even waste—you first wash them thoroughly before embracing them and letting them sit on your lap. In the same way, God sees us covered in the stain of sin. Only the divine, life-giving blood of Jesus has the power to cleanse us and restore us to our rightful place with God. And it is only through faith in the sanctifying sacrifice of Jesus that we are made clean and righteous in the sight of God.

What is sin?

It's one of the most important questions you can ask. At its core, sin is separation from God—the true source of life and purpose. Sin creates a distance between us and God's presence, cutting us off from the life He intended for us to live.

Isaiah 59:2 states, *But your iniquities have separated you from your God; your sins have hidden His face from you, so that He will not hear.*

Romans 3:23 states, *For all have sinned and fall short of the glory of God.*

John 15:5 states, *I am the vine; you are the branches. If you remain in me and I in you, you will bear much fruit; apart from me, you can do nothing.*

For most people, the word *sin* is often misunderstood and misinterpreted. Only God's Word reveals its true meaning, exposing its origin, cause, and sin's power over humanity.

For the past 30 years, I have experienced the undeniable power of God's Word. His Word is alive and active, sharper than a double-edged sword, piercing deep into our hearts and souls. It exposes our thoughts, motives, and intentions, leaving nothing hidden. God's Word reveals the truth within us and transforms us from the inside out (Hebrews 4:12).

Ancient roots and the origin of sin

Through my spiritual awakening, I came to understand the reality of God's adversary—Satan. He is not just a symbol of evil or a myth, but a real spiritual being who actively opposes God and all that is good. Satan is actively working to keep people in spiritual darkness, blinding them from seeing the truth and experiencing the grace of God (2 Corinthians 4:4).

The Bible describes Satan as "the father of lies" (John 8:44) and "the deceiver of the whole world" (Revelation 12:9). He is the enemy of humanity, working to separate people from God through lies, temptation, and destruction (1 Peter 5:8).

The Scriptures reveal the origin and rebellion of Satan in the heavenly realms. God created Lucifer as a glorious and powerful angel (Ezekiel 28:12–15; Isaiah 14:12–14). Though these passages originally address earthly kings, they are often understood as referring to Satan's pride and rebellion against God (Isaiah 14:13–14). Because of his rebellion, Lucifer was cast out of heaven (Revelation 12:7–9) and became Satan—the enemy of God and all that is good (Revelation 12:9).

Yet, the good news is this: Jesus Christ defeated Satan through His death and resurrection. Though Satan still tries to deceive and destroy, his power is limited. One day, God will bring final judgment, and Satan will be destroyed forever (Revelation 20:10).

Satan's primary goal is to keep people separated from God, using lies, deception, and false beliefs to lead them away from the truth. He tempts people to live independently of God, convincing them to trust in themselves, other gods, or philosophies instead of the Creator.

Satan's main weapon is deception. He blinds people to the truth about God's love and salvation. I'm sharing this because understanding who Satan is helps us understand why the world is broken, why people are searching, and why the message of Jesus is so important.

But the Good news is that the Bible makes it clear:

Satan has already been defeated by Jesus Christ through His death and resurrection.

Satan's final judgment is certain, and his power is limited.

Jesus came to destroy the works of Satan and to set people free from his lies and control.

The Bible calls Satan the "father of lies" (John 8:44) and warns that he masquerades as an angel of light (2 Corinthians 11:14), often appearing attractive but always leading people away from truth and life.

Is Karma Real?

Karma is a Sanskrit term meaning 'action' or 'deed.' In Hinduism and Buddhism, it refers to the belief that a person's actions determine their future experiences, including rebirth. The Bible affirms a moral law of sowing and reaping—our actions have real consequences—but rejects reincarnation. Instead, Scripture teaches that each person lives once, dies once, and then faces judgment before God. Our eternal destiny isn't determined by balancing good and bad deeds, but by whether we have received God's gift of salvation through faith in Jesus Christ.

Hebrews 9:27 says *People are destined to die once, and after that to face judgment.*

No amount of "good karma" can cleanse sin—only the **sacrificial death and resurrection of Jesus** provide forgiveness and reconciliation with God.

Karma is a deceptive human philosophy that rejects God's grace and the complete salvation Jesus offers. It keeps people trapped in striving, guilt, fear, and spiritual deception.

I was raised to see life through the lens of karma, believing that my actions dictated my experiences and future outcomes. It seemed natural to accept that every deed—good or bad—would return in kind, shaping my destiny. However, during a season of deep life crises, I began to reflect and question this understanding.

By the grace of God, I came to a life-changing realisation: Jesus (Yeshua) did come to shine the light on the deceptive belief. The Bible reveals that we are not trapped in an endless system of earning and repaying consequences. Instead, through the sacrifice of Yeshua on the cross, He bore the punishment for our sins, offering us freedom, grace, and a new beginning.

I want to remind you again what Ephesians 2:8-9 declares:

> *For it is by grace you have been saved, through faith— and this is not from yourselves, it is the gift of God— not by works, so that no one can boast.*

Unlike karma, which **demands repayment for every wrong, Jesus offers forgiveness and redemption.** His mercy lifts the burden of our past, not our efforts. This truth set me free—I no longer had to strive endlessly to balance the scales. **Through faith in Christ, I received not what I deserved but what He lovingly gave: eternal life and a restored relationship with God.**

First-century theologian Paul writes in Romans 8:1-2

> *There is now no condemnation for those who are in Christ Jesus because, through Christ Jesus, the law of the Spirit who gives life has set you free from the law of sin and death.*

In Yeshua, we are freed from the cycle of cause and effect that karma represents. His sacrifice offers a new life, grounded not in fear of punishment for past deeds but in the grace and redemption that He freely gives.

Instead of living under the weight of our past actions, we are invited to walk in the light of God's mercy. 2 Corinthians 5:17 says, *If anyone is in Christ, the new creation has come: The old has gone, the new is here!*

Through Jesus Christ, I have come to understand life in a new way—not as something bound by fate or human effort, but as a life transformed by God's grace. In Him, we find true freedom, knowing that our future is no longer determined by past mistakes, but shaped by His boundless love and divine purpose.

The Cross of Yeshua (Jesus) has broken the power of sin and death for all who believe in Him (Romans 6:9-10). It is the only way to restore our relationship with our Creator God, offering redemption, forgiveness, and the promise of everlasting life and peace (Colossians 1:20, John 14:27).

In my search for truth, I discovered that the Bible reveals a far greater reality than any man-made philosophy. While millions are deceived into believing they must earn a better life through their actions, God's Word declares that salvation is a gift of grace, received through faith in Jesus

Christ alone. Though Scripture acknowledges the principle of sowing and reaping (Galatians 6:7), it does not teach an endless cycle of repayment or reincarnation. Instead, the Bible offers true redemption through Christ, who bore the punishment we deserved and set us free from the power of sin and condemnation (Romans 8:1-2).

True justice and transformation do not come through human effort, religious rituals, or moral striving. They come only through God's love, mercy, and grace. Unlike karma, which traps people in an endless cycle of cause and effect, Jesus Christ offers complete forgiveness, a new identity as children of God (John 1:12), and the promise of eternal life (John 3:16).

Through Scripture, I've come to see karma as a man-made false system based on works, lacking true redemption. While the Bible affirms personal responsibility (Galatians 6:7-8), it reveals a higher truth: God's mercy triumphs over judgment (James 2:13). Unlike reincarnation or endless repayment cycles, the Bible teaches that Christ's atonement offers complete forgiveness and freedom from sin's eternal consequences (Hebrews 9:27-28).

God's truth surpasses all human philosophies. His ways are higher (Isaiah 55:8-9), and Jesus Himself declared: *"I am the way, the truth, and the life. No one comes to the Father except through Me"* (John 14:6). Salvation comes not by human effort but by God's grace through faith in Christ (Ephesians 2:8-9). At the Cross, Jesus defeated sin and death, breaking the curse over humanity. This is the divine exchange: our brokenness for His wholeness, our despair for His hope.

All have sinned and fallen short of God's glory (Romans 3:23). I realised my pride and ignorance kept me believing I had to earn salvation. But Romans 10:9 makes it clear: *If you declare with your mouth, "Jesus is*

Lord," and believe in your heart God raised Him from the dead, you will be saved. Salvation is not earned but received through faith in Christ alone.

I no longer seek Moksha (Salvation) through cycles of rebirth. The moment I placed my faith in Jesus, I was freed from sin and death (Romans 8:1-2). While the Bible teaches sowing and reaping, it also reveals God's mercy and grace, offering eternal life through Christ.

Jesus affirms this powerful truth about our salvation in John 14:6, saying, **I am the way, the truth, and the life. No one comes to the Father except through Me.**

The Bible provided me with a higher moral framework than karma. While actions have consequences, God's grace offers redemption. *Taste and see that the Lord is good* (Psalm 34:8). Like John Newton, who found God's amazing grace and helped abolish the slave trade, we are called to live in gratitude and purpose.

Karma teaches an impersonal system of justice, but the Bible reveals a personal, loving God who extends mercy and forgiveness through Christ. We are not trapped in endless cycles but are given new life in Him (2 Corinthians 5:17).

I also discovered that the Bible rejects caste and social hierarchies. *There is neither Jew nor Gentile, slave nor free, male nor female, for you are all one in Christ Jesus* (Galatians 3:28). God shows no favouritism (Acts 10:34-35). His justice includes care for the vulnerable (Isaiah 1:17).

While Karma emphasises personal responsibility, the Bible offers God's grace. Even Gandhi was inspired by Jesus' words on nonviolence (Matthew 5:39), reflecting biblical principles of peace and justice (Romans 12:19-21).

Social reformers like Basaveshwara promoted moral living, but the Ten Commandments, given by God through Moses, carry divine authority for all people and all times. God's laws offer not only moral guidance but also the invitation to a relationship with Him.

Despite reform movements, caste discrimination persists. The Bible proclaims that God reconciles all people through Christ, creating one new humanity (Ephesians 2:14-16). While both karma and Scripture emphasise accountability, only the Bible reveals grace through Christ, offering forgiveness that karma cannot.

Remember that it is our sin that separates us from God. It's not just wrong actions but a heart condition. Only through Jesus' sacrifice can we be truly freed from sin and receive eternal life. God's forgiveness liberates us from guilt and condemnation, transforming our hearts.

Imagine God paying the price for all your sins—this is what Jesus did at the Cross. Our good deeds become a response to grace, not a way to earn salvation (Micah 6:8).

Concepts of karma enslave you, but faith in Christ sets us free. *The thief comes to steal, kill, and destroy; I have come that they may have life, and have it to the full* (John 10:10).

Jesus paid it all (Hebrews 10:10, John 19:30), and there is no reincarnation—just the offer of eternal life through faith.

God's Word, sharper than any sword (Hebrews 4:12), reveals our hearts and brings healing and renewal. Just as an MRI diagnosis of hidden disease, Scripture exposes our deepest need and leads us to life in Christ.

Conclusion:

Growing up, I often heard my parents attribute our hardships to "bad karma," a common belief in our culture that suffering results from past actions. Like many, I once believed this philosophy that bound people in fear and striving. But I discovered that karma is a man-made belief that denies God's grace and the salvation found in Jesus Christ. The Bible reveals that sin, not karma, is the true cause of separation from God (Isaiah 59:2). Sin blinds our hearts and keeps us from the freedom that Christ offers. Life isn't about luck or fate; everything happens under God's sovereign plan (Proverbs 16:33, Romans 8:28). While many think life is random, the Bible teaches that God controls every detail for His purpose.

Through a life-changing encounter with Jesus, I learned that only His sacrifice can cleanse us from sin and restore our relationship with God (John 3:3). Unlike karma, which teaches endless repayment, Jesus offers complete forgiveness and new life (Ephesians 2:8-9). Karma keeps people in fear and guilt; Jesus frees us to live in His love and grace. Scripture shows that Satan deceives the world and uses lies to keep people from God (John 8:44; 2 Corinthians 4:4). But Jesus defeated Satan through His death and resurrection (Revelation 12:9), offering us victory and hope.

The Bible reveals true justice and transformation come through Christ's sacrifice, not human effort. Romans 3:23 reminds us that all have sinned, but Romans 10:9 promises salvation to those who believe in Jesus. Karma enslaves, but Jesus liberates. Through faith in Him, we become a new creation (2 Corinthians 5:17), no longer bound by guilt and condemnation (Romans 8:1 2). Salvation is not earned by works but received as a gift of grace (Ephesians 2:8-9). Jesus is the way, the truth, and the life (John 14:6). In Him, I found true freedom and the promise of eternal life.

Living the Message: Practical Questions

1. Are there areas in your life where you feel burdened by guilt or fear of past actions? How can you surrender them to God's grace?

   _____
   _____
   _____

2. How does understanding God's love and forgiveness challenge your view of justice and mercy?

   _____
   _____
   _____

3. What steps can you take to live with purpose and share the freedom found in Jesus with others?

   _____
   _____
   _____

CHAPTER 6

Early Childhood of the Sunrise Baby

Behold, I have given you authority to tread on serpents and scorpions and over all the enemy's power, and nothing shall hurt you. Luke 10:1

A Scorpion-Snatching Baby!

As I reflect on my life, from birth to where I stand today, I see a narrative woven with divine interventions—moments where God's miraculous hand shielded me from the dangers that sought to take my life.

The shadows of death, as I once mentioned, have lingered since the very beginning, but time and again, God has lifted me from the depths of peril. As I look back, I marvel at the many miracles that filled my life, and now, I wish to share with you some of the key moments that revealed the depths of God's grace and protection over me.

The first story comes from my earliest years when I was just a baby—barely old enough to understand the dangers around me, yet already walking through the valley of death. South India, where I was born, is known for its abundant wildlife, including some of the world's deadliest scorpions and snakes. These creatures were not uncommon, and tragically, many lives had been lost over the years to their venomous bites and stings.

When I was about nine months old, my parents told me that I had already begun crawling all over the house, eager to explore the world around me with the innocent curiosity of a child. My elder sister, who was around ten years old at the time, later recounted the story in greater detail. She recalled how neighbourhood doctors rushed over to attend to my emergency.

A Fearless Faith

One day, however, my crawling curiosity led me to a deadly encounter. I spotted a slow-moving creature on the floor, and without any fear or knowledge of its lethal power, I crawled toward it and grasped it in my tiny hands. It was a large scorpion, one of the most venomous creatures in the region.

The scorpion struck me, injecting its deadly venom into my arm. I screamed, and my parents rushed into the room, horrified by what they saw. They knew the deadly consequences that could follow such a sting. The venom quickly began spreading through my arm, and panic set in. Soon, doctors from nearby rushed into our home, desperately trying to save my life. I was too young to remember the details of how they treated me, but I was later told that I had come very close to death.

In the late 1960s, scorpion stings were a significant public health concern in South India, particularly in rural areas. While precise statistics from that time are scarce, it is estimated that thousands of children were affected by scorpion stings annually, especially in regions with high scorpion populations, such as Tamil Nadu, Karnataka, and Andhra Pradesh.

During that period, the fatality rate for scorpion stings was reported to be relatively high, particularly among children. The rate varied between 5% to 30% depending on the severity of the envenomation, access to medical care, and the species of scorpion. The most dangerous scorpions in South India were species of the genus *Mesobuthus* and *Hottentotta*, known for their potent venom.

Children, due to their smaller body mass, were particularly vulnerable to severe symptoms, and fatalities were often caused by cardiovascular complications like pulmonary edema and heart failure. These complications could set in hours after the sting if proper medical care was not received.

At that time, medical interventions were limited, especially in rural areas, and specific antivenoms were not always readily available.

Another Miracle

It was a miracle that I survived. The Word of God revealed more mysteries about my near-death encounters. For years, I had forgotten about that terrifying incident. But one day, as I was reading the Word of God, a particular verse in the Gospel of Luke stirred my memory. Jesus, speaking to His disciples, said

> *I have given you authority to trample on snakes and scorpions and to overcome all the power of the enemy; nothing will harm you.* Luke 10:19

At that moment, I was flooded with awe and wonder. This verse reminded me of that childhood encounter with the deadly scorpion, and I suddenly saw that moment through a new lens—the lens of God's protection and grace.

I realised that what had happened to me all those years ago was not just an accident or a random escape from death. It was a testimony to God's faithfulness and mercy. He had preserved my life, even as a baby, so that I could one day stand here and proclaim His goodness. It wasn't just about survival; it was about purpose. God had spared me so that I might walk in His calling and share His miraculous grace with others.

The Bible is filled with reminders of God's power over the forces that seek to harm us. Psalm 91:13 says,

> *You will tread on the lion and the cobra; you will trample the great lion and the serpent.*

This scripture speaks of the authority and protection that God grants to those who trust in Him. It is not that we won't face dangers, trials, or moments where death feels close, but it is the assurance that in those moments, God is our protector, our shield, and our deliverer.

As David declares in Psalm 23:4

> *Even though I walk through the darkest valley, I will fear no evil, for you are with me; your rod and your staff, they comfort me.*

In my life, there have been many valleys of death—times when I passed through shadows so dark that only the light of God's mercy could pull me through. That scorpion's sting was just one of the many moments when God intervened, sparing me from harm for reasons I would only understand later in life. His protection over me was not by chance but part of His plan for my life.

What strikes me most is that God, in His infinite love, not only protected me from physical harm but has continually protected my spirit from the sting of the enemy. Just as Jesus spoke of scorpions and serpents as symbols of the enemy's power, I now see that the physical dangers I faced as a child mirrored the spiritual battles we all face. *The enemy seeks to steal, kill, and destroy, but Jesus came so that we might have life and have it abundantly.* John 10:10

I marvel at how God, in His sovereignty, has carried me through. My life is a testimony of His saving power—not just from physical harm but from the spiritual forces that seek to bring death to our souls. When I think back on that moment with the scorpion, I see it now as a symbol of the countless ways God protects us, even when we are unaware. His hand has been over my life from the beginning, and He continues to lead me, just as He leads all of us who trust Him.

So, I share this story not just to recount a moment of danger but to give glory to the God who delivers and who saves. He is the same yesterday, today, and forever. If you find yourself walking through your valley of death—whether it be physical danger, emotional pain, or spiritual attack—know that God is with you. His power is greater than any force that seeks to harm you, and His purpose for your life will stand, just as it has for mine.

I have seen His mercy firsthand, and I know that His protection is available to all who call upon His name. The shadow of death may loom, but the light of God's grace will always prevail.

As you reflect on your life through the lenses of God's Word, you may begin to recognise the many divine interventions that have shaped your journey. Just as David the Psalmist pondered in awe of the grace and mercy that followed him all the days of his life, so too can you experience the revelation of God's rich love and faithful presence. The Great Shepherd, who tenderly watches over every step of your path, longs to reveal His unfailing love to you in deeper ways than you may have imagined.

Consider Psalm 23:1,4

> *The Lord is my shepherd; I shall not want... Even though I walk through the valley of the shadow of death, I will fear no evil, for You are with me; Your rod and Your staff, they comfort me.*

This timeless truth serves as an invitation to meditate on God's continual presence, even in the darkest and most challenging moments. His guidance is sure, His comfort is constant, and His love is unfathomable.

I share this with you not only to recount moments of danger or trial but to give glory to the God who delivers, the God who saves. He is the same yesterday, today, and forever.

His character is unwavering, and His promises remain true through every season of life. If you find yourself walking through your valley of the shadow of death—whether through physical danger, emotional turmoil, or spiritual battles—take heart. Know that God is with you, and His presence is your refuge. Hebrews 13:8 says *Jesus is the same yesterday and today and forever.*

Meditate on this: the power of God is greater than any force that seeks to harm you, and His purpose for your life will stand firm, just as it has for mine. In the face of trials, fear, or uncertainty, we can rest in the assurance that God's protective hand is upon us, shielding us from harm and guiding us toward His perfect will.

I have seen His mercy firsthand, and I stand as a witness to His protection and love, which is available to all who call upon His name. The valley may seem long, and the shadow of death may loom large, but remember this: the light of God's grace will always prevail. As *Psalm 91:1* declares, *He who dwells in the shelter of the Most High will rest in the shadow of the Almighty.* I will never forget that in His shadow, there is peace, protection, and abundant provision.

Take time today to ponder these truths. Reflect on how God's hand has been upon your life, even in ways you may not have seen before. Invite Him to open your eyes to the divine interventions that have marked your journey, and trust that His faithfulness will continue to guide you forward.

His grace will follow you, His love will sustain you, and His light will lead you through every valley.

A Salty Child

Another dangerous childhood experience my parents often reminded me of was my peculiar love for chewing salty rocks. Back in those days, cooking salt didn't come in fine grains like we see today, but rather in large rock-like pebbles. I would grab a handful in my small left hand and quietly wander outside, savouring each salty piece as I chewed. It was an innocent habit, but it quickly became a dangerous one fateful day.

On that day, as I was happily munching on the salty rocks, one large piece suddenly lodged in my throat. In an instant, I began to choke. I gasped for air, struggling as my breath became shallow, and I was unable to speak. My parents, watching in horror, didn't know what to do. Panic filled the air. In that terrifying moment, when it seemed there was no way out, a quick-thinking woman from the neighbourhood rushed over. With wisdom and calm, she bent my head forward and gave a few firm, quick blows to the back of my neck. And just like that, the choking rock was dislodged, and my life was spared.

As I reflect on that moment now, it reminds me of God's mercy in the most unexpected circumstances. What could have ended in tragedy was turned into a moment of deliverance, not by my strength or knowledge, but through the intervention of someone else and, ultimately, by the grace of God.

This childhood memory is more than just a story of a near-death experience; it is a reminder of God's constant protection over our lives. In Matthew 5:13, Jesus tells us,

> You are the salt of the earth. But if the salt loses its saltiness, how can it be made salty again?

As I think of my literal love for salt, I'm reminded of the deeper spiritual truth in these words. Salt preserves, purifies, and enhances. In the same way, we are called to preserve God's truth, purify the world through our witness, and enhance the lives of those around us by pointing them to Christ.

But just as I once choked on that salt pebble, sometimes the things we cling to can become stumbling blocks. The good things in life, when misused or placed out of context, can cause us to choke spiritually. We can find ourselves gasping for spiritual breath, caught in situations where we feel helpless. Yet, even in those moments of distress, God is faithful to deliver us, just as He did that day in my childhood. Psalm 34:17 reminds us.

> *The righteous cry out, and the Lord hears them; He delivers them from all their troubles.*

I now see that moment as a picture of God's mercy and grace. I could do nothing to save myself—I was completely dependent on the intervention of someone else. In the same way, there are many times in our spiritual lives when we cannot save ourselves. We choke on the cares of this world, on sin, or on the things we think will bring satisfaction. But God, in His mercy, steps in. As Psalm 116:8 says,

> *For You, Lord, have delivered me from death, my eyes from tears, my feet from stumbling.*

He bends down, just as that neighbour did, and rescues us from the things that threaten to overwhelm us.

This experience also brings to mind the mercy and grace found in Jesus. We, too, have been rescued from something far more dangerous than a choking rock. Romans 6:23 reminds us,

> *For the wages of sin is death, but the gift of God is eternal life in Christ Jesus our Lord.*

Sin, like that rock, can block the life-giving breath of God's Spirit in us. But Jesus, in His love, has provided the way out. Through His death and resurrection, He has given us freedom from sin's grip, and He restores us to life, just as I was restored to breathe again that day.

As I look back on this event and connect it to the Word of God, I am reminded that we are called to be salt to the world. However, we must be careful not to lose our saltiness and not to let the things of this world cause us to choke spiritually. It's easy to become so focused on worldly desires, habits, or distractions that we lose sight of our true purpose. But God, in His kindness, is always there to guide us back, to purify us, and to give us new life.

So, let this memory inspire you to reflect on your own life. Are there areas where you feel spiritually 'choked'—where something is blocking the flow of God's presence and grace in your life? Are there 'salty rocks' you are holding onto that may seem harmless but are dangerous to your spiritual health?

Take time to meditate on these words from Colossians 4:6,

> *Let your conversation be always full of grace, seasoned with salt, so that you may know how to answer everyone.*

As the salt of the earth, we are called to reflect God's grace in our lives. Let us pray that our lives remain full of the true salt that preserves, heals, and brings life to others. Others may taste and see that the Lord our God is indeed Good and Gracious.

Finally, take heart in knowing that just as God delivered me from that choking rock, He will deliver you from any spiritual obstacle. His mercy is new every morning, and His grace is sufficient to sustain you. Trust in His guidance, and know that the One who saves is always near. His hand is never too short to rescue, and His love never fails.

Reflecting on this childhood memory, it's hard not to see the deeper spiritual parallel. Just as I unknowingly craved those salty rocks, how often do we crave things that seem satisfying but, in the long run, may harm us? The world offers many things that seem appealing, but they cannot truly satisfy the deep hunger in our souls. We may not realise it at the time, but God is always gently guiding us, protecting us from the things we don't yet understand.

Jesus spoke of salt in a much different way. In Matthew 5:13, He said, *You are the salt of the earth. But if the salt loses its saltiness, how can it be made salty again? It is no longer good for anything except to be thrown out and trampled underfoot.*

Here, Jesus uses salt as a symbol of something far greater—our calling as believers to preserve, flavour, and bring healing and restoration into a world that is spiritually decaying. Salt, when used properly, is valuable. It purifies, preserves, and enhances. But when we lose our 'saltiness', our purpose and our effectiveness in God's Kingdom begin to fade.

As you ponder this, consider how God has preserved you. Just as my parents carefully watched over me, preventing me from making decisions that could harm me, God watches over us. His Word says in Psalm 121:7-8, *The Lord will keep you from all harm—He will watch over your life; the Lord will watch over your coming and going both now and forevermore.*

Even in our innocence, naivety, or wandering, God's hand is upon us, guiding us back to safety and protecting us from unseen dangers.

Perhaps there are areas in your life where you've unknowingly been reaching for 'salty rocks'—things that seem harmless, even satisfying, but could lead you down a path away from God's best. It's easy to get caught up in what feels good at the moment, but Jesus reminds us that true satisfaction comes not from worldly desires but from being aligned with God's will.

In John 4:13-14, Jesus told the woman at the well the following.

> *Everyone who drinks this water will be thirsty again, but whoever drinks the water I give them will never*

> *thirst. Indeed, the water I give them will become in them a spring of water welling up to eternal life.*

His living water is what truly satisfies, not the temporary pleasures or distractions of this world.

So, as you reflect on this childhood memory, let it serve as an invitation to examine your life. Where are you reaching for 'salty rocks' when God is offering you the richness of His grace, the fullness of His love? Let this be a moment to recalibrate, to ask the Holy Spirit to reveal any areas where your spiritual 'saltiness' has faded, where you've settled for less than what God has for you.

A Truth Meditate

Just as my parents protected me from those dangerous pebbles, God can lead you toward a life filled with purpose, meaning, and true satisfaction. He is the Good Shepherd, watching over every step of your journey. Take time today to seek His face, to ask for His guidance, and to rest in the assurance that His plans for you are good, as Jeremiah 29:11 reminds us:

> *For I know the plans I have for you, declares the Lord, plans to prosper you and not to harm you, plans to give you hope and a future.*

Remember, the salt of God's Word will preserve you from corruption, His living water will sustain you in the deserts, and His love will always guide you toward a purpose-driven life. Even when you are tempted to reach for something less, His plans exceed our limited understanding. Let the new sunrise lead you to taste and see that the Lord is Good.

> *No weapon forged against you will prevail, and you will refute every tongue that accuses you. This is the heritage of the servants of the Lord, and this is their vindication from me, declares the Lord.* Isaiah 54:17

Conclusion

Reflecting on my life, I see a narrative of divine interventions where God's hand has shielded me from harm. As a nine-month-old baby, I had a life-threatening encounter with a venomous scorpion in South India. Despite being stung, God miraculously spared my life through the quick actions of local doctors. Decades later, while reading Luke 10:19, *I have given you authority to trample on snakes and scorpions…nothing will harm you.* I realised that my survival wasn't a mere chance but part of God's divine purpose for my life.

Another childhood memory recalls my peculiar love for chewing salty rocks, which nearly ended in tragedy when one lodged in my throat. A neighbour intervened just in time, saving my life. This incident, too, reminds me of God's mercy and how He delivers us even when we are unaware of the dangers surrounding us.

These moments reveal profound spiritual truths. The scorpion symbolises not only physical danger but also spiritual battles, while the choking salt pebble reflects how earthly desires can obstruct our spiritual growth. Yet, God's grace preserves and restores us, offering protection from harm and spiritual stagnation.

Psalm 23:4 and 91:13 reassure us that God is our shepherd and deliverer, guiding us through the valleys of life. Jesus' words in Matthew 5:13 remind us of our calling to be *the salt of the earth*, reflecting His love and purpose to a world in need.

Through these stories, I see God's faithfulness in preserving me for a greater purpose. I share this testimony to encourage you: no matter the valley you face, trust in God's unfailing love and protection. He is with you, offering grace, guidance, and the assurance of His sovereign plans for your life.

Living the Message: Practical Questions

1. How has God protected you from dangers or challenges that you initially did not recognise as divine interventions?
   _____
   _____
   _____

2. Are there "salty rocks" in your life, habits or desires that seem harmless but hinder your spiritual growth? How can you surrender them to God?
   _____
   _____
   _____

3. In what ways can you embrace your role as the "salt of the earth," preserving and reflecting God's love and truth to those around you?
   _____
   _____
   _____

CHAPTER 7

A Tender Sunrise and Success

The fear of the Lord is the beginning of knowledge; fools despise wisdom and instruction. Proverbs 1:7

Nurtured by Knowledge:
Childhood Immersed in Learning

My childhood was filled with memories that I cherish deeply, memories that shaped who I am today. Growing up in a household where both my parents were college and high school teachers meant that education and knowledge were highly valued. Books were more than just objects in our homes—they were windows into new worlds, sources of wonder, and tools for expanding our minds. My parents actively encouraged us to read, explore, and learn, and our efforts were always rewarded.

I still remember being engrossed in stories that carried me to far-off lands, worlds that existed beyond the boundaries of my small town. Those stories inspired me in ways I didn't fully understand at the time, but God was already planting dreams in my heart.

My parents were unknowingly setting the foundation for the journey God had planned for me, nurturing a curiosity that would lead to future adventures beyond anything I could imagine.

A Surprising Achievement: Storytelling

At the age of 12, I participated in a regional story-writing competition. I wrote the best I could, pouring my imagination into words, never expecting anything remarkable. To my surprise, I won first prize! And a silver medal to reward my success. It was an achievement that humbled me and gave me a sense of wonder about the gift God had given me—the ability to express thoughts, ideas, and emotions through stories.

That first prize wasn't just a certificate or a medal—it was a reminder that God's plans for me were unfolding in ways I couldn't see yet. He had placed a love for storytelling in my heart and was using it to shape my future.

I didn't realise it at the time, but God was shaping my life through those little moments of success. Each achievement, no matter how small, was part of a bigger plan. Just like it says in Jeremiah 29:11 *For I know the plans I have for you, declares the Lord, plans to prosper you and not to harm you, plans to give you hope and a future.*

This verse is a beautiful reminder that God has a unique plan for every person on this planet. He wants to see us thrive and live with purpose. Unfortunately, it makes me sad to think that many people don't recognise or believe in such a wonderful promise from God.

Imagine if everyone understood that they are part of something greater! The Bible also tells us in Romans 8:28 that *all things work together for the good of those who love Him.*

This means that even when things seem difficult or confusing, God is still at work behind the scenes, weaving together our experiences for our benefit.

When I think about the flowers in a garden, each one is unique, yet they all contribute to the beauty of the garden. Similarly, we each have our path, and every success, every failure, and every moment shapes us into who we are meant to be. In God's grand garden, we all have a unique part to play. The Holy Bible offers us God's divine plan for life to all who believe and obey.

So, if you find yourself feeling lost or uncertain, remember that you are not alone. God is with you, guiding you toward your future. Embrace the small successes and trust that they are part of a larger journey.

I am always encouraged by Philippians 1:6, it is written that *He who began a good work in you will carry it on to completion until the day of Christ Jesus.*

This verse reassures us that God is continually working in our lives, and He will bring His plans to fruition.

Let this knowledge inspire you! Let this understanding enlarge your capacity to see God with a new mindset. No matter where you come from or what challenges you face, God has a beautiful plan for you. Trust in Him, and you will discover the hope and future He has in store.

As I was writing this story, I was reminded of James 1:17 *Every perfect gift is from above, coming down from the Father of the heavenly lights, who does not change like shifting shadows.*

This verse teaches us that God's intentions are always good, aligning with Jeremiah's message of hope and future blessings.

A Vision Beyond Borders: Expanding My Worldview

My father had a unique way of opening our eyes to the wider world. He subscribed to international magazines like National Geographic and SPAN, which transported me to places and cultures far beyond the borders of my small town. The colourful images and fascinating stories about different countries began to stir something inside me. I started to dream of travelling to these distant lands, of exploring the vast world that existed beyond what I knew.

God's Exceeding Abundance: Dreams Fulfilled in Unexpected Ways

I remember watching commercial jumbo jet planes cruising over our town's skies, and I would tell my friends, "One day, I would love to travel in that plane and go to a distant land". It was a childish dream, something that seemed impossible at the time. After all, no one in our family or town had ever flown on an aeroplane. But in my heart, I kept that desire alive. I now see that God planted a dream in my heart, even as a child. Psalm 37:4 teaches us to *Delight yourself in the Lord, and He will give you the desires of your heart.*

I didn't realise it back then, but God was listening to my childlike dreams and planning to fulfil them in ways I could never have imagined. Not only did my dreams come true, but God exceeded my expectations beyond anything I could think or envision. As it says in Ephesians 3:20, *Now to Him who can do exceedingly abundantly above all that we ask or think.*

Throughout my life, I've had the incredible opportunity to travel to many countries and explore major cities around the world. God even opened a remarkable door for me to work for a large airline, which allowed me to travel with my family across the globe. This experience has been nothing short of amazing!

What I once considered a big dream in my childhood turned out to be a way for God to show His limitless goodness in my life. Let me encourage you to dream like a child and meditate on Psalm 37:4, which says *Delight yourself also in the Lord, and He shall give you the desires of your heart.*

God's plans for us are often bigger and more beautiful than we can imagine. When we dare to dream and trust Him, He leads us on extraordinary journeys filled with blessings we never thought possible.

Years later, I look back and realise how God, in His faithfulness, has brought me far beyond what I ever imagined as a child. What seemed like a distant, impossible dream—the idea of flying and travelling to far-off lands—became a reality. Through opportunities and blessings, I was able to travel, explore new places, and see the world in ways I could not have anticipated.

God has fulfilled that childhood dream of mine, not because of anything I did, but because of His goodness and grace. It's a reminder that when we walk in His ways, *no good thing does He withhold from those whose walk is blameless.* Psalm 84:11

Opportunities that Expanded My Horizons

As I continued to grow, God opened even more doors. My academic achievements continued to surprise me again. In my final year of high school, I ranked first in my local region, another achievement that filled me with both surprise and humility. These weren't just accomplishments; they were moments where God was preparing me for the greater plans He had in store.

My father also played a pivotal role in broadening my world. I'll never forget when he surprised me by taking me to the big city of Mumbai to watch a Cricket Test match when I was just 13. That experience was beyond anything I could have hoped for, filling me with a sense of excitement and wonder about life beyond my small town. Whether it was through family trips, school excursions, or summer holidays with relatives, each experience added to my desire to explore the world around me.

Just as Proverbs 16:9 explains, *In their hearts, humans plan their course, but the Lord establishes their steps.* I may have had dreams and plans, but it was God who guided my steps and allowed me to experience things beyond my imagination.

Challenge and Reflection: Trusting God's Plans

As I reflect on these early memories, I am amazed at how God's hand was over my life even when I didn't realise it. The dreams I held as a child, the accomplishments I didn't expect, and the opportunities that broadened my world were all part of His intricate design for my life.

I want to encourage you today to think about your own life—about the dreams, desires, and unexpected blessings that have come your way. Sometimes, we think that our dreams are too far-fetched or too impossible. But God is a God who does the impossible. He is a God who is not limited by our circumstances or the world around us. As Isaiah 55:8-9 reminds us, *For my thoughts are not your thoughts, neither are your ways my ways, declares the Lord. As the heavens are higher than the earth, so are my ways higher than your ways and my thoughts higher than your thoughts.*

Take time to reflect on how God may be working in your life, even in ways you can't see. What dreams has He placed in your heart? Are you trusting Him to fulfil them in His time and in His way? Are you learning to delight in Him and His Word?

Meditation: Walking in Faith

Spend time meditating on Ephesians 3:20.

> *God can do 'immeasurably more' than all we can ask or imagine. As you think about the desires of your heart, remember that God is faithful, and His plans for you are good. He may lead you through unexpected paths, but He will never withhold any good thing from those who walk according to His ways.*

Let this truth sink into your heart, *no good thing will He withhold from those who walk uprightly.* Psalm 84:11

Trust in God's timing, and allow Him to guide you into the abundant life He has prepared for you.

Childhood Filled With Sports and Passion

One of the most cherished memories from my childhood was the joy of playing sports, particularly cricket and table tennis. These sports were not just games; they were an integral part of my life and my family and friendship culture. With older brothers and friends who shared my love for these activities, I was introduced to them at an early age.

We would play in the streets, under the blazing sun, without shoes, hats, or even sunscreen. The heat never bothered us because our hearts were full of passion, joy, and excitement. Those moments were filled with endless energy and uncontainable enthusiasm as we ran, shouted, and played with everything we had. I naturally became quite good at these sports and soon I was elected as the Captain of my school's cricket team.

By the time I was 13, I had played numerous competitive matches, sometimes opening the batting and sometimes opening the bowling. We travelled as a team to nearby towns for tournaments, inviting other teams to our hometown as well. For us, it felt like playing in international Test matches. Looking back now, I realise that these experiences shaped my social and leadership skills—building qualities of teamwork, resilience, and courage. Yet, as I would later discover, these childhood games and experiences were also a window into a deeper, spiritual reality.

God is Always at Work

Many of our life experiences guide us toward knowing God and accepting His incredible gift of grace and mercy. Every challenge we face and every joy we experience are opportunities to draw closer to Him.

Romans 8:28 reminds us, *And we know that in all things God works for the good of those who love Him.* This means that God is always at work in our lives, using our experiences for our ultimate good.

When we see life as an opportunity to grow and connect with God, we begin to recognise His grace as a constant source of strength and His mercy as a welcoming embrace. By opening our hearts to these lessons, we can deepen our relationship with Him and truly understand His love.

Childhood Dreams And Divine Lessons

Years passed, and I found myself immersed in the Word of God, gaining new insights into life and faith. One day, as part of my daily routine, I was reading the Gospel of John, specifically Chapter 4. This chapter recounts the story of Jesus' encounter with a Samaritan woman at a well. This woman was an outcast due to her lifestyle. In this profound conversation, Jesus reveals to her the true nature of worship. He states in John 4:24,

> *God is Spirit, and those who worship Him must worship in spirit and truth.*

I was puzzled by this statement. Until that moment, my understanding of worship was limited to what we did at church—singing songs, clapping hands, raising our hands and participating in corporate gatherings. But here, Jesus was speaking of a different kind of worship, one that went beyond traditional actions. In that moment of meditation, I asked God to help me understand what it truly means to 'worship in spirit and truth.'

To my surprise, God brought to mind a vivid memory from my childhood—a memory that I had long forgotten.

The Forgotten Dream and Its Meaning

As a child, I was so passionate about cricket that, even after the game had ended for the day, my mind would still be consumed with it. I remember waking up in the middle of the night, screaming and shouting as though I was still on the field. I would be yelling in my sleep, 'How was that…?'

Asking for an LBW (Leg Before Wicket) decision from the umpire in my dreams. My mother, gently tapping me on the shoulder, would whisper, "Son, your game is over… please go back to sleep".

These dreams were frequent during my childhood, and I had forgotten all about them until this particular moment of meditation. I began to ask God what this dream had to do with worshipping Him in spirit and truth. I thought that there was nothing spiritual about my childhood dreams and games. Then, my mind opened to a divine revelation.

God impressed upon my heart a profound insight. Just as my mind and spirit were fully engaged with the game, even while my body was asleep, 'True worship is a deep engagement of our spirit with God's presence', even beyond the external actions of worship. My body was at rest, but my spirit was still actively engaged in playing the game. In the same way, worship in spirit is an ongoing connection with God, a heart posture that transcends physical actions and outward expressions.

This realisation brought the verse to life.

> *God is a spirit, and His worshipers must worship in spirit and truth.* John 4:24

Worship is not limited to a church service or a scheduled time; it's about a continued engagement of the heart, mind, and spirit with the Spirit of the living God. Just as I remained immersed in cricket even after the game was over, I can remain in communion with God throughout the day, worshipping Him in everything I do, whether I'm aware of it or not.

A Deeper Understanding of Worship

That seemingly forgotten childhood dream had suddenly taken on new meaning. It reminded me that worship isn't about following a strict set of rituals or traditions but about living in constant awareness of God's presence. Worshipping in spirit and truth means engaging with God from the depth of our being, where our spirit longs to be united with His Spirit.

I was reminded of Romans 12:1, which says,

> *Therefore, I urge you, brothers and sisters, given God's mercy, to offer your bodies as a living sacrifice, holy and pleasing to God—this is your true and proper worship.*

Worship, in its truest form, is about offering our entire lives to God—our thoughts, desires, dreams, and actions—as an act of gratitude and surrender to His will.

My childhood passion for cricket and those vivid dreams became a divine illustration of how 'True Worship' is about being fully absorbed in God's presence, where our spirit is constantly engaged with Him, even when we are not actively doing something religious.

Reflection: Living in Continuous Worship

As I reflect on this lesson, I am deeply moved by how God can use even the most unexpected memories to teach us profound spiritual truths. The passion and joy I felt playing cricket as a child now serve as a reminder of how I should approach my relationship with God, with that same enthusiasm, joy, and wholehearted engagement.

What about you?

Are there parts of your life—whether in childhood memories or everyday routines—that God is using to draw you closer to Him?

Have you thought about how your heart can remain engaged in worship even outside of traditional settings?

Let this be a reminder that true worship is not confined to church buildings or temples or at specific times of the week. It's about living in continuous communion with God, where our hearts are always open to His presence, His love, and His truth. There are no mornings without the Sunrise.

It is written in Lamentations 3:22-23

> *Because of the Lord's great love, we are not consumed, for his compassion never fails. They are new every morning; great is your faithfulness.*

God's mercies are renewed with every sunrise, symbolising hope and fresh beginnings each day. As one wise man said, "Yesterday is history, tomorrow is a mystery, but today is a gift. That is why it is called "present".

Do not let this gift be wasted through ignorance of truth. Consider Psalm 113:3, *From the rising of the sun to the place where it sets, the name of the Lord is to be praised.*

This verse calls for continuous worship, acknowledging God from sunrise to sunset.

Colossians 3:17 encourages us:

> *And whatever you do, whether in word or deed, do it all in the name of the Lord Jesus, giving thanks to God the Father through Him.*

This is the essence of worship in spirit and truth—to live each moment for the glory of God, whether we are at work, at play, or in quiet reflection.

Meditation: Engaging with God Beyond the Moment

Spend some time meditating on John 4:24—*worshipping God in spirit and truth.* Ask God to help you recognise areas of your life where you can invite His presence and live in a state of continuous worship.

Remember that just as I was absorbed in the game long after it ended, we can be absorbed in God's presence long after the church service is over. He invites us into an unceasing relationship, where every moment is an opportunity to engage with His love and grace.

Let this truth transform the way you view worship. It's not about rituals—it's about relationships. And just as God used a childhood passion of mine to reveal a profound truth, He can use your own life experiences to draw you closer to Him if you're willing to listen and engage with His Spirit.

> *Because of the tender mercy of our God, by which the rising sun will come to us from heaven to shine on those living in darkness and the shadow of death, to guide our feet into the path of peace.* Luke 1:78-79

Conclusion

My childhood was filled with the joy of learning, a love for storytelling, and an early awareness of God's guiding hand through dreams and life experiences. Growing up in a home of educators, I was surrounded by books that fueled my curiosity and inspired dreams of far-off lands. This foundation of learning was complemented by moments where I could sense God shaping my life in ways I hadn't expected.

At the age of 12, I won a storytelling competition—an affirmation that creativity was a gift God had placed within me. Looking back, I can see how God was preparing me for a greater purpose. As Jeremiah 29:11 reminds us, *For I know the plans I have for you, declares the Lord, plans to prosper you and not to harm you, plans to give you hope and a future.* While this promise was originally given to Israel, it reflects the heart of God toward His people—His plans are always for good, leading us toward hope in Him.

My father's love for learning and his broad worldview expanded my horizons. Through magazines like National Geographic and trips to big cities, he instilled in me a desire for adventure and discovery. Childhood dreams, like travelling on a jumbo jet, seemed impossible in our small-town life. Yet, Psalm 37:4 says,

> *Delight yourself also in the Lord, and He shall give you the desires of your heart.*

As I sought to follow God, He shaped my desires and graciously opened doors I never imagined—allowing me to work for an airline and travel the world.

Even my passion for cricket became a way God taught me deeper truths. Reflecting on how absorbed I was in the game, I realised how true worship—described in **John 4:24** as *worshipping in spirit and truth*—calls for a heart fully engaged with God, far beyond external actions or moments of emotion.

Through life's successes, fulfilled dreams, and simple everyday joys, I now see how God orchestrates each step of our journey. His plans are often beyond what we could imagine, and even the smallest moments—like childhood dreams—can reveal His presence and purpose. As we trust Him, He leads us into the abundant life He has prepared for us in Christ (John 10:10).

Living the Message: Practical Questions

1. What childhood dreams or passions has God fulfilled in your life, and how have they revealed His greater purpose for you?

   _____
   _____
   _____

2. Are you living in a state of continuous worship, engaging your heart and spirit with God beyond traditional religious practices?

   _____
   _____
   _____

3. How can you align your current dreams with God's promises, trusting Him to exceed your expectations in His perfect timing?

   _____
   _____
   _____

CHAPTER 8

An Exodus: A Sunset for A New Sunrise

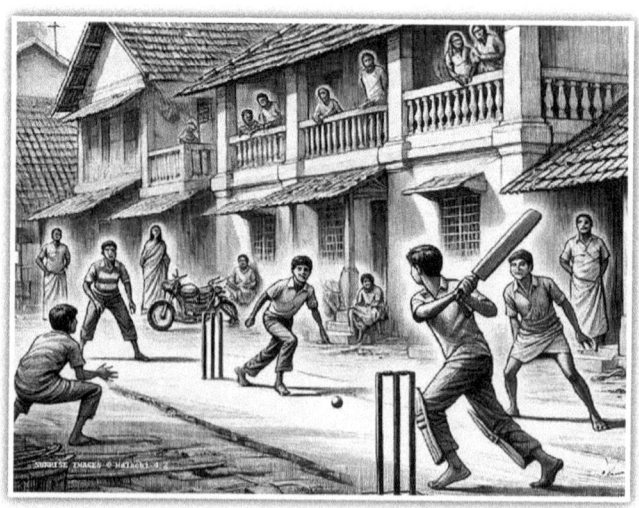

And the Lord went before them by day in a pillar of cloud to lead them along the way, and by night in a pillar of fire to give them light, that they might travel by day and by night. Exodus 13:21

AN EXODUS: A SUNSET FOR A NEW SUNRISE

A Divine Destiny

After finishing high school with top grades and preparing to start my Engineering Degree, I was enjoying summer break with my friends. We spent our days playing cricket, and I looked forward to studying in the same town where my father was a respected professor at a local college. Everything seemed perfect, and my future was going as planned. But God was about to change my path in a way I never expected.

The Unexpected Change

One afternoon, amid a fun game with friends, my parents called me into the house. They asked me to sit down, which felt unusual since most of our conversations were informal. My father started the conversation by saying, "We've been thinking about your higher education. We believe it would be better for you to move to a bigger city like Bengaluru. Your elder brother is already working there, and with your top grades, you'll have the chance to attend some of the best universities.

What do you think?"

I was caught off guard. The idea of leaving my hometown, the only place I had ever called home, felt daunting. The thought of living in a bustling city like Bengaluru excited me, but the reality of leaving my parents, friends, and everything I knew was overwhelming. I was comfortable where I was—just like the Israelites who, even after escaping Egypt, yearned to go back rather than face the unknown wilderness ahead.

It was a tough choice. I knew I had to think carefully about what this opportunity meant for my future. Would stepping out of my comfort zone lead to new adventures and experiences, or would it just bring anxiety and loneliness?

Hoping that my parents would forget about the idea, I replied, "If you think it's a good idea, I'll consider going." I tried to rush back to my game, but my parents called me back. My father said, "Why don't you start packing your bags now? There's an express bus in five hours."

I was shocked. Suddenly, I realised that my parents wanted me to leave that very day. The safety of my home, the love of my family, and the company of my friends were slipping away. The familiar comforts of my life were being replaced by the fear of the unknown.

I wanted to speak up, share my worries, and cry—but I couldn't find the words. My parents thought my silence meant I agreed, but inside, I felt torn. Even with all these emotions, I chose to respect my parents' decision.

Stepping Out in Faith

Reluctantly, I agreed to my parents' request. With a heavy heart, I said goodbye to my friends, packed my bags, and prepared for the long journey. I didn't realise it at the time, but that moment marked the beginning of a new chapter—a chapter that would ultimately lead me to God's promised land for my life.

Much like the Israelites' exodus from Egypt, I was being led into the unknown. But God was with me every step of the way, just as He promised in Deuteronomy 31:8: *The Lord himself goes before you and will be with you; he will never leave you nor forsake you. Do not be afraid; do not be discouraged.*

As I boarded that bus that night, I didn't know what lay ahead, but I trusted in my parents' decision, knowing that an unseen power was guiding my path.

The Blessings of Obedience

What I once viewed as a painful separation from my comfort zone turned out to be the beginning of a journey toward fulfilment and purpose. My time in Bengaluru opened doors I could never have imagined. I studied at one of the best universities, developed lifelong friendships, and grew in ways I wouldn't have if I had stayed in my small town. Looking back, I realised that God was preparing me for something greater—just as He led the Israelites through the wilderness to the Promised Land.

I continued to excel in my studies and sporting activities. I was elected to represent the student body at the college sporting events. This opportunity gave me the influence to inspire many of my friends to take part in annual sporting competitions. Some of my friends still remember that moment with immense gratitude.

Isaiah 55:8-9 reminds me, *For my thoughts are not your thoughts, neither are your ways my ways,' declares the Lord. As the heavens are higher than the earth, so are my ways higher than your ways and my thoughts higher than your thoughts.* Even when we don't understand God's plans, we can trust that He is always leading us toward something good.

Trusting in God's Plan

Later in life, I was reminded of Jeremiah 29:11 *For I know the plans I have for you, declares the Lord, plans to prosper you and not to harm you, plans to give you hope and a future.*

Even though I couldn't see it at the time, God was leading me to my promised land.

Reflecting on my journey, I now understand the importance of stepping out in faith and trusting that God has something greater for me.

Each significant moment in my life, even those that seemed insignificant at the time, was part of God's plan to lead me to where I am today.

Proverbs 3:5-6 reminds us to *trust in the Lord with all our heart and lean not on your understanding; in all your ways submit to him, and he will make your paths straight.*

When we begin to open our eyes to the possibility that nothing is accidental, we can start to see God's hand at work in ways we never imagined. Life becomes less about chance and more about trusting the One who knows us better than we know ourselves, the One who has a plan for us that is good and purposeful.

A Divine Appointment

I once believed life was ruled by accidents—random twists of fate shaped by bad luck or karma. Everything felt unpredictable, and even good events seemed like mere coincidences without deeper meaning. But as I reflected on my life, I realised that many pivotal moments were far from accidental. They were divine appointments—purposeful events guided by a force beyond coincidence.

I came to understand that God's hand was at work, directing my steps even when I was unaware. As Proverbs 16:9 says, *In their hearts, humans plan their course, but the Lord establishes their steps.* What seemed random was part of a greater plan that God had for my life.

One such divine appointment happened on what seemed like a regular weekend in Bangalore. Typically, I expected nothing extraordinary—just visiting friends or watching a movie. But during this particular weekend, something profound occurred.

My brother-in-law had a close family friend preparing to migrate to the USA. Out of respect, my wife and I decided to visit him to say our goodbyes. Though I had never met this man before, I agreed to accompany my wife, not expecting more than a friendly conversation. This encounter, however, was anything but ordinary.

Upon our arrival, this person—a stranger to me at that time—took an unusual interest in me. He asked about my life, plans, and dreams. At the time, I had no clear vision for my future. His questions made me ponder aspects of my life I hadn't yet explored, as though a door was opening that I hadn't known existed.

When he asked about my plans, I mentioned that I was considering migrating to Australia or Canada. This simple response became the turning point of my life. The man looked at me thoughtfully and said, "Australia? Wait a moment." He returned with an application form for Australian permanent residency, explaining that he had picked up extra forms during a recent visit to the Australian High Commission in Delhi. "This one may be for you!" he said with a smile.

At that moment, I felt like time had stopped. Here was a man I had never met, offering an opportunity that would shape my entire life. It was clear this was no accident—this was a divine appointment arranged long before I was aware.

A few weeks later, I filled out the form and sent it to the Australian High Commission. This simple act set in motion a series of events that eventually led me to migrate to Australia. Looking back, I see how that moment was a divinely orchestrated meeting that changed the course of my life.

What I once believed to be coincidences or accidents, I now recognise as carefully designed moments of destiny. Romans 8:28 reminds us, *And we know that in all things God works for the good of those who love him, who have been called according to his purpose.*

Each of us experiences these divine appointments—moments that usher us into new chapters of our lives. Often, these moments appear as ordinary encounters or casual conversations, but they are turning points in our stories.

When we open our eyes to the possibility that nothing is accidental, we see God's hand at work in ways we never imagined. Life becomes less about chance and more about trusting the One who knows us better than we know ourselves, the One with a good and purposeful plan for us. See Jeremiah 29:11.

A Miracle Called Merlyn

My next nine years in Bengaluru were filled with numerous challenges. Travelling to university was tough, especially with my health issues caused by heavy pollution. The loneliness I felt often threatened to derail my dreams. Yet, I pushed through these struggles and faced various family challenges head-on.

Despite the obstacles, I completed two engineering diplomas and a management diploma in just seven years while working full-time. During this journey, I encountered yet another major miracle—Merlyn. Our meeting at college and our subsequent marriage felt nothing short of miraculous.

Proverbs 18:22 says,

> *He who finds a wife finds what is good and receives favour from the Lord.*

In the biblical context, marriage is portrayed as a covenant that enriches both partners spiritually, emotionally, and practically. This has profound implications for our lives.

Marriage: A Divine Gift for Fulfilling God's Purpose

Marriage is not merely a social contract but a profound gift from God, designed to fulfil His plan and purpose for our lives. From the very beginning, God demonstrated the beauty of companionship when He said in Genesis 2:18, *It is not good for the man to be alone; I will make a helper suitable for him.*

Just as Adam needed Eve to accomplish God's greater vision for humanity, I have come to see that my marriage is a precious blessing from the Creator Himself, tailored to His divine purpose.

God, in His wisdom, is the ultimate matchmaker for those who place their trust in Him. He may not give us a 'perfect' spouse, but He blesses us with the **right one**—the one who complements us, adds value to our lives, and helps us grow in ways we could never achieve alone. A godly spouse becomes a partner in life's journey, where strengths and weaknesses are balanced in mutual love, patience, and humility.

Marriage is not about finding someone to complete us but rather someone with whom we can fulfil God's calling together. The joy and challenges of marriage serve as a refining process, shaping us into the people God intended us to be. In this sacred bond, we learn the essence of grace, forgiveness, and sacrificial love—the very attributes that mirror Christ's love for the Church.

A Christ-centered marriage bears fruit—not only in terms of raising a family but also in terms of nurturing spiritual growth, character, and purpose. In this union, we are called to be fruitful, not just biologically but also in cultivating joy, peace, and goodness that glorify God. Together, as husband and wife, we reflect the divine partnership that advances God's kingdom here on earth.

When we trust God with our hearts and desires, He writes a story that far surpasses our expectations. He aligns our lives with someone who will walk with us through life's seasons—someone to laugh with, to pray with, and to lean on when life's burdens feel heavy. This divine partnership is a reminder that we are not meant to journey alone but to walk hand in hand with the one whom God has chosen for us, fulfilling His beautiful design for marriage.

In trusting God as the author of our love story, we see that His plan is always good and purposeful. Our spouses may not be "perfect" by worldly standards, but in God's hands, they are perfect for us—helping us grow, become fruitful, and live out His glorious purpose as individuals and as one.

Four practical applications have greatly helped me.

1. **Valuing Relationships:** Appreciate the commitment and companionship in marriage. If you're in a marriage, seek to nurture it, recognising it as a source of goodness and mutual support.
2. **Intentional Partnership** Choosing a partner wisely is crucial. Look beyond superficial traits and consider qualities that align with values, purpose, and mutual respect. Building a strong relationship involves intentionality, patience, and care.
3. **Recognising God's Favour** See marriage as a space where God's blessings can manifest. Even through life's difficulties,

shared growth, understanding, and support make the marriage journey a uniquely divine partnership.
4. **Encouraging Others** The word of God emphasises the importance of seeking a meaningful, godly relationship for those who are not yet married. For those who are, it serves as a reminder to cultivate a relationship built on mutual growth, love, and respect, creating an environment where both partners can thrive.

The book of Proverbs is both a reminder of the goodness found in marriage and a call to honour that gift with intention, gratitude, and commitment.

I was also blessed with a great job as Deputy Manager for Design and Development at a company exporting precision products to the USA and Europe. During this time, my dreams started to take shape. By my eleventh year in Bengaluru, God graciously opened the door to my Promised Land—Australia.

Reflect and Trust

As you reflect on your own life, I challenge you to ponder the moments that may have seemed like coincidences or accidents. Could they have been divine appointments, leading you toward something greater? Take time to meditate on how God might be guiding your steps, even in the smallest details.

Through my journey, I've learned to trust that God is in control even when I don't have all the answers. Every significant moment is part of a greater plan that leads to purpose and fulfilment. In your own life, consider how God might be directing your path and trust that, just as He has carefully designed each of my steps, He is doing the same for you. Let this knowledge inspire you to step forward with faith, knowing that every moment holds meaning in the hands of the One who loves you deeply.

Conclusion

As a high school graduate preparing to study engineering, I was enjoying a carefree summer, looking forward to what seemed like a straightforward path. Then, unexpectedly, my parents asked me to leave our small town that very evening to move to the big city of Bengaluru, where I could pursue higher education at top universities. The suddenness of the decision felt overwhelming. Leaving behind my familiar comforts, friends, and family for an uncertain future reminded me of the Israelites' journey into the wilderness, where they had to trust God's unseen plan.

Despite my hesitation, I respected my parents' decision—unaware at the time that this step of obedience would become a turning point in my life.

In Bengaluru, I faced many challenges: pollution that affected my health, loneliness, and family struggles. Yet, by God's grace, I persevered. Over the years, I completed two engineering diplomas and a management diploma while working full-time. During this journey, I met Merlyn, my wife, a true miracle and blessing who brought immense joy into my life. Eventually, I secured a prestigious position as Deputy Manager in a company exporting precision products internationally.

Then came another divine appointment—a chance conversation with a stranger that led to an opportunity to apply for Australian permanent residency. This unexpected moment reshaped my future and revealed how God was orchestrating every detail of my life in ways I could never have planned on my own.

Looking back, what once seemed like a painful detour was God leading me to my promised land, just as He promised in Jeremiah 29:11:

> *For I know the plans I have for you, declares the Lord, plans to prosper you and not to harm you, plans to give you hope and a future.*

Through obedience, faith, and trust in His greater plan, I have experienced blessings, personal growth, and opportunities beyond anything I could have imagined. Truly, God's ways are higher than ours (Isaiah 55:8-9), and His plans are always purposeful and filled with hope.

Living the Message: Practical Questions

1. Are there areas in your life where God may be calling you to step out of your comfort zone and trust His plans?
   _____
   _____
   _____

2. How can obedience to God and others in authority lead to unexpected blessings in your life?
   _____
   _____
   _____

3. Reflecting on your life, can you identify any "divine appointments" where God orchestrated events for your good?
   _____
   _____
   _____

Every great dream begins with a dreamer. Always remember that you have within you the strength, patience, and passion to reach for the stars and change the world.
Harriet Tubman.

CHAPTER 9

A Sunrise in the Promised Land

> *Arise, shine, for your light has come,*
> *and the glory of the Lord rises upon you.*
> *See, darkness covers the earth,*
> *and thick darkness is over the peoples,*
> *But the Lord rises upon you,*
> *And his glory appears over you.*
> Isaiah 60:1-2

Dreaming of a Distant Land

I have come to understand that dreams are often viewed as messages from God in the Bible.

In biblical history, dreams often served as divine messages from God to guide, warn, or reveal His plans. They reflect God's communication with humanity, allowing insights to emerge that shape our direction in life. Scripture presents dreams as profound tools for spiritual guidance and connection:

> **Job 33:14-15** *For God does speak—now one way, now another—though no one perceives it. In a dream, in a vision of the night, when deep sleep falls on people as they slumber in their beds.*

Meaning: God uses dreams to reach us when we are most still and receptive.

> **Genesis 40:8** *They said to him, 'We both had dreams, but there is no one to interpret them.' Then Joseph said*

> to them, 'Do not interpretations belong to God? Tell me your dreams.'

Meaning: True understanding of dreams comes from God, as seen through Joseph's God-given gift.

> **Joel 2:28** *And afterward, I will pour out my Spirit on all people. Your sons and daughters will prophesy, your old men will dream dreams, and your young men will see visions.*

Meaning: Dreams are a manifestation of God's closeness and willingness to guide His people.

These verses highlight God's desire to lead us through dreams, unveiling truths and directions that bring clarity and purpose to our lives.

A Childhood Dream Fulfilled

As a child, I dreamed of travelling to a distant land, never imagining how this dream would become a reality. Years later, when I received my Permanent Residence visa to Australia, I marvelled at the miracles God had performed in my life.

During the visa application process, I struggled to gather the funds needed. For six months, I waited, placing the application booklet under my pillow at night. I dreamt repeatedly of flying in a Boeing 747 and landing in Australia, surrounded by vast wheat fields ready for harvest. These dreams instilled hope, reminding me that God is my Shepherd (Psalm 23:1), providing for me even when I didn't fully know Him.

Eventually, God's provision came through, often in unexpected ways—mentors who taught me skills, opportunities to build confidence, and financial breakthroughs. Looking back, I see how God orchestrated every step.

The Wheat Field and God's Harvest

The recurring vision of the wheat field became more than a symbol of hope. Over time, I understood its deeper significance. Jesus said, *The harvest is plentiful, but the labourers are few* Matthew 9:37.

The wheat field represented the spiritual harvest—the many souls ready to receive God's love but waiting for workers to share the Gospel.

This realisation humbled me. My journey to Australia wasn't just about fulfilling personal dreams; it was about serving a higher purpose. God had called me to be a labourer in His field, sharing His love with those around me.

John 4:35 reminded me to *open your eyes and look at the fields! They are ripe for harvest.* My life's blessings, challenges, and opportunities were all part of God's divine plan to use me for His glory.

Ephesians 2:10 declares, *For we are God's handiwork, created in Christ Jesus to do good works, which God prepared in advance for us to do.*

God doesn't just fulfil our needs—He calls us to participate in His greater mission. When we trust Him like a child trusts their father, He invites us into a life of purpose and impact.

A Prophetic Prayer and God's Provision

As I prepared to leave for Australia, my brother-in-law prayed over me, asking for God's provision and guidance, particularly for employment.

At the time, I found this strange, as I didn't think prayer could influence such practical matters. However, this prayer would later reveal God's faithfulness.

Upon arriving in Australia during a severe economic recession, I faced a daunting job market. Yet, within a week, I secured employment—a miracle that affirmed God's hand over my journey. Philippians 4:19 declares, *And my God will meet all your needs according to the riches of His glory in Christ Jesus.* God's provision came precisely when I needed it most.

When my first job ended 18 months later, I faced uncertainty again. However, through prayer and community support, God led me to a new opportunity. These experiences deepened my understanding of His faithfulness, teaching me to rely on Him for guidance and provision.

Navigating Change with Faith and Perseverance

Adjusting to life in Australia was both an exciting and challenging journey for my wife and me. One of the biggest hurdles we faced was adapting to the culture and understanding spoken English. The Australian accent, with its unique expressions and speed, was initially difficult to grasp. Determined to improve, I began listening to ABC Radio and cricket commentary—a beloved pastime in Australia. Immersing myself in these broadcasts not only sharpened my listening skills but also helped me communicate more effectively.

Of course, my Indian accent often added moments of humour. Sometimes, people playfully joked about my pronunciation during conversations and speeches. I chose to laugh along, knowing that humour can bridge cultural gaps and create connections.

For my wife, the most challenging part was finding her first job. Despite her skills and qualifications, she sent countless applications with little to no response. It was a disheartening time. One day, however, a friend gave her a piece of advice that changed everything: "Why not volunteer your time at an organisation that could benefit from your expertise?"

Following this wise suggestion, my wife began volunteering at a local organisation where her talents were greatly appreciated. Her dedication and hard work did not go unnoticed. In time, a vacancy opened up, and she was offered a paid position. What began as an act of faith blossomed into a rewarding opportunity.

Her volunteer work was like sowing seeds in faith, trusting that God's promises would come to fruition. As the Bible says:

> *Do not be deceived: God cannot be mocked. A man reaps what he sows.* Galatians 6:7

This experience reminded us that when we sow seeds of kindness, perseverance, and faith, we can trust God to provide the harvest in His perfect time. What felt like a setback became a testament to God's faithfulness and provision.

Spiritual Awakening in Sydney

My wife encouraged me to attend a local church, where I began participating in Bible study groups. Through their joyful worship and warm fellowship, I encountered God's love in unexpected ways. The group's energy and the simple act of singing, *This is the day the Lord has made*

Psalm 118:24, awakened a curiosity in me: Who is this God that brings such joy?

Again, Jeremiah 29:11 reminded me of God's plans for hope and a future. Slowly, I realised that the challenges and blessings I had experienced were all part of His plan to draw me closer to Him.

Restoration Through God's Grace

One of the most challenging moments of my journey was receiving a letter from my father, expressing his heartbreak over my decision to marry a Christian woman. He declared that I was no longer his son. This rejection shook me, but my wife reassured me that God would one day restore our relationship.

Romans 6:11 spoke to me: *Count yourselves dead to sin but alive to God in Christ Jesus.* Over time, I witnessed God's transformative power in my father's life. Through His grace, our relationship was restored, a testament to Romans 8:28, *And we know that in all things God works for the good of those who love him.*

The Ministry of Reconciliation

Years later, when my father suffered a stroke, I felt a deep call to share the Gospel with my parents. Guided by 2 Corinthians 5:18, which speaks of the ministry of reconciliation, I focused on helping them find peace with God, not through "conversion," but through a restored relationship. By God's grace, both my parents embraced Jesus as their Saviour, becoming new creations in Christ. Their transformation was a beautiful reminder of God's power to heal and redeem.

Beauty for Ashes

The **Ashes Series** is one of the fiercest and most historic rivalries in cricket—a battle for pride between Australia and England, etched in history with unforgettable moments of victory and loss.

But, I discovered that beyond the game, the **Bible tells a far greater story**—a story of how God brings **beauty from ashes**, turning our deepest losses into lasting victories. While nations compete for a trophy made from ashes, God offers us **a crown of beauty,** hope, and new life.

As Isaiah 61:3 says, *To give them beauty for ashes, the oil of joy for mourning, the garment of praise for the spirit of heaviness.*

Beauty for Vibhuti

I grew up in South India, where our family practised many deeply rooted spiritual traditions. One of the most significant was the application of **Vibhuti**—sacred ash, also known as *Bhasma*. After taking a bath, we reverently applied Vibhuti to the forehead as three horizontal lines, *Tripundra*, symbolising purity, detachment, and devotion to God. This daily ritual served as a constant reminder of life's transient nature and the importance of humility and surrender.

Applying Vibhuti was intended to be an expression of reverence and humility, aligning my soul with the divine through a physical act of repentance. Yet, for me, it remained an outward ritual, lacking the deeper inner transformation that true surrender brings.

Interestingly, I found a striking similarity in the traditions of Australian Aboriginal cultures. During ceremonies and rituals, they paint their bodies using natural pigments like ochre, charcoal, and clay. These intricate designs—often on the forehead and hands—convey more than artistry; they represent social status, spiritual beliefs, familial bonds, and a deep connection to the land and their ancestors. While the application of Vibhuti is a personal act of devotion, Aboriginal body painting is often communal, strengthening cultural identity and collective memory.

Both practices share profound spiritual significance. The ashes remind the devotees of their mortality and the need to surrender to God's will, while the Aboriginal people believe that these designs connect individuals to ancestral spirits and the Dreamtime—the spiritual dimension of creation and belonging.

In South Indian culture, Vibhuti represents religious identity and personal piety, an outward sign of inward humility. Similarly, Aboriginal body painting serves as a living story passed down through generations, preserving their connection to heritage and spiritual beliefs.

But it was through the word of God that I understood the true meaning behind the application of ashes and the profound power of God's grace.

In many other traditions, ashes symbolise mourning and humility—a physical expression of inner sorrow and repentance. But in biblical times, ashes represented grief and loss, yet God's promise in Isaiah 61:3 reveals a beautiful reversal: mourning would be replaced by joy. The exchange of a *crown of beauty for ashes* is a powerful wordplay in Hebrew, underscoring God's ability to transform brokenness into glory.

This same passage speaks of the *oil of gladness*—an anointing that symbolised divine blessing and renewal, as reflected in Psalms 45:8 and 133:2. An anointed face was more than a sign of favour; it signified spiritual restoration and joy, demonstrating the fullness of life that comes from walking in God's grace.

Embracing Australia's Cultural Tapestry

Living in Australia allowed me to appreciate its rich cultural diversity, particularly the heritage of Aboriginal Australians. Psalm 24:1 declares *The earth is the Lord's, and everything in it.* Recognising the connection Aboriginal people have to the land enriched my understanding of stewardship and respect for creation.

A few years ago, while living in Sydney, my cousin from South India visited us. To make their trip memorable, we embarked on a road trip along the scenic Pacific Highway to Narooma, renowned for its stunning beaches and rich Aboriginal history.

One highlight was visiting the Umbarra Aboriginal Cultural Centre, where we delved into Aboriginal traditions. Storytelling, wood art, and ancient hunting techniques brought their culture vividly to life. My cousin eagerly tried a spear-like hunting tool, aiming at a target, while I captured photos of the moment.

Then, something extraordinary struck me. Standing next to the Aboriginal guide, my cousin's facial features bore an uncanny resemblance to the guide's. It was startling. Could it be that, separated by continents and millennia, there was a shared ancestry between us?

Modern research suggests intriguing connections between Australia's Indigenous peoples and South India's Dravidian communities—echoes of ancient migrations and shared origins. This realisation transformed our cultural tour into a profound reflection on humanity's interconnectedness.

It brought to mind Acts 17:26 *From one man He made all the nations… and He marked out their appointed times in history and the boundaries of their lands.*

This verse underscores our shared humanity—one family created by God, uniquely spread across the earth yet united by His design.

That day, Narooma became more than a destination; it became a reminder of the intricate tapestry of humanity. What began as a simple road trip evolved into a spiritual revelation—an affirmation that, despite our differences, we are all threads in the same divine story authored by God.

Great Southland of the Holy Spirit

Some time ago, I uncovered a fascinating and significant truth about Australian history—one that has been largely overlooked or suppressed by mainstream media and the education system. This truth is vital for every generation to understand, as it aligns with the identity and destiny of Australia as the Great Southland of the Holy Spirit.

Pedro Fernández de Quirós, a Portuguese navigator serving Spain, made an extraordinary proclamation in 1606. On May 14, 1606, during the feast of Pentecost, Quirós landed on an island in what is now Vanuatu, believing it to be part of the mythical southern continent, Terra Australis. There, he declared:

"Let the heavens, the earth, the waters with all their creatures and all those here present witness that I, Captain Pedro Fernandez de Quiros... in the name of Jesus Christ... hoist this emblem of the Holy Cross... on this day of Pentecost, 14 May 1606... I take possession of all this part of the South as far as the pole in the name of Jesus... which from now on shall be called the Southern land of the Holy Ghost... and this always and forever... and to the end that to all natives, in all the said lands, the holy and sacred evangel may be preached zealously and openly."

This declaration resonates with Australia's spiritual heritage and calls for its recognition as a land set apart for God. Understanding and embracing this profound truth can inspire Australians to seek a deeper sense of identity and purpose, anchored in the destiny proclaimed over this land more than 400 years ago.

This historical insight invites all Australians to reflect on their spiritual heritage and recognise the nation's unique identity as a Great Land of the Holy Spirit.

A Divine Builder

My family moved from Sydney to Brisbane in the year 2005, seeking a fresh start. We planned to settle down and buy a home, but being new to the city, we decided to rent for six months to get a feel for the area. During that time, we started house hunting, meeting real estate agents, attending open houses, and putting in offers. But to our disappointment, some agents were less than honest, and we lost a few opportunities.

Frustrated, I remembered Psalm 127 *Unless the Lord builds the house, the builder's labour is in vain.* I held onto this verse, turning it into a prayer with my wife and our teenage daughter. We wrote the scripture on a piece of paper and prayed over it, asking God for a home in a specific area, free from the hassle of unethical agents.

Then God gave me an idea: create a flyer!

With Psalm 127 at the top, I wrote that I was a genuine buyer looking for a private sale, included my contact details, printed 40 copies, and placed them in letterboxes around the neighbourhoods we loved. Though we didn't get any immediate response, I felt peace knowing I'd followed God's lead.

A few weeks later, on a weekend house hunt, we decided to explore some streets we hadn't visited yet. My wife suggested we check out a particular street—a closed road with only one way in and out. At the end, we saw a sign: Private Sale. Thrilled, we called the owner, who told us the house had been on the market for a few weeks. He'd already lowered the price and was eager to sell.

We thanked God and toured the home. After a brief negotiation, we agreed on a price with a handshake and a small deposit—all in under 40 minutes. I've shared this story with many, encouraging them to trust God's promises, especially Psalm 127. God exceeded every expectation we had, and we moved into an almost new home.

I encourage you to trust the Lord wholeheartedly for your needs.

Tune your heart to His voice, follow where He leads, and never forget—sometimes, your miracle is just a few steps away, waiting on the path called "Obedience".

Conclusion

Dreams have often served as a medium through which God communicates His will, offering guidance, revelation, and encouragement. Biblical accounts, such as Joseph's interpretation of dreams (Genesis 40:8) and Joel's prophecy of spiritual dreams (Joel 2:28), emphasise their significance in revealing God's plans. Similarly, in my own life, dreams of travelling to a distant land became a reality far beyond my expectations when God orchestrated my journey to Australia.

I vividly recall a period when financial constraints made it impossible to submit my visa application. Night after night, I dreamed of landing in a Boeing 747 surrounded by golden wheat fields. At the time, I didn't fully grasp the spiritual significance of these dreams. Years later, reflecting on Matthew 9:37, I realised that the wheat field symbolised the spiritual harvest—souls ready to receive God's love but awaiting labourers to share His message. This revelation transformed my perspective: my move to Australia wasn't merely for personal success but for a greater purpose in God's kingdom.

Through countless challenges, including financial struggles and cultural adjustments, God remained faithful, providing mentors, opportunities, and resources. In His perfect timing, He fulfilled my childhood dream, showing me that trust and childlike faith open doors to divine blessings.

As Jesus reminds us in John 4:35, *Open your eyes and look at the fields! They are ripe for harvest.* My journey to Australia became not just about my success but about becoming a labourer in God's harvest, sharing His love and truth. It's a calling we all share—to trust God, step into His plans, and participate in His greater purpose for our lives. Let the divine Architect build your life step by step.

Living the Message: Practical Questions

1. How do you interpret dreams or desires in your life—could they be God's way of guiding you toward His plans?

   _____
   _____
   _____

2. What comfort zones might you need to leave to trust God's greater purpose for your life?

   _____
   _____
   _____

3. How can you become a labourer in God's spiritual harvest, sharing His love with those around you?

   _____
   _____
   _____

> A God-sized dream is never just about you. It's about fulfilling God's purpose for you so that, through you, He can reach others.
>
> *Mark Batterson.*

CHAPTER 10

A Sunrise Over Shadows of Sin

The heart is deceitful above all things and beyond cure. Who can understand it?

A Sunrise Over My Sins

We are all born with a nature that leans toward selfishness; no one needs to teach children how to demand attention, cry for their desires, or manipulate those around them. The Bible reminds us of the inherent deceitfulness of our hearts in Jeremiah 17:9 *The heart is deceitful above all things and beyond cure. Who can understand it?* This verse highlights the natural inclination toward selfishness that exists within us from a young age.

I once heard a powerful analogy that beautifully illustrates how God longs to wash away our sins, much like a parent desires to keep their baby clean. Imagine your baby is covered in a mess, wearing stinky and soiled clothes. Your first instinct is to wash and clean the baby—you wouldn't take the baby to the bedroom or living room until they are thoroughly cleaned.

In the same way, when we come to God with our broken, guilty, and messy lives, His first desire is to cleanse us and make us whole. However, many resist His invitation, choosing instead to remain in their filthy condition, often blaming God or others for their situation. God's arms are always open, ready to clean and restore us, but we must take the step to let Him.

In an earlier chapter, I shared how I was nurtured by knowledge, with my parents actively encouraging us to read. They instilled in me a love for learning, which I am grateful for. However, I also found myself exposed to books from older friends and my older brother that were not suitable for a 12-year-old. My fleshly nature was drawn to these books, believing that reading them would help me mature faster than my peers.

This secretive reading eventually came to my father's attention, and the disciplinary action that followed was severe. In my anger, I lashed out at my older brother, who was only a year and a half older than me, mistakenly directing my frustration towards him instead of addressing my actions. My parents had warned us strictly against reading inappropriate materials, but at that moment, I felt justified in my rebellion.

Looking back on this incident, I realise that we are all born with sinful and selfish natures, as David states in Psalm 51:5 *Surely, I was sinful at birth, sinful from the time my mother conceived me.* This acknowledgment of our inherent nature is crucial for understanding our need for redemption.

The remedy for such a condition lies in God's incredible gift of a new heart and mind. In Ezekiel 36:26, God promises, *I will give you a new heart and put a new spirit in you; I will remove from you your heart of stone and give you a heart of flesh.* This transformation is essential for overcoming our natural inclinations and becoming who God created us to be.

Through His grace, we can be renewed and empowered to live a life that reflects His love and righteousness. The journey of faith is not just about recognising our flaws but embracing the transformative power of God's Spirit, which enables us to rise above our selfish tendencies and strive for a life of purpose and compassion.

Power of our Traditions

As I look back on my journey, I realise how much my upbringing was shaped by traditions and rituals deeply rooted in South Indian culture. From an early age, I participated in the feast days and celebrations dedicated to many gods, observing practices passed down through generations. In my family, we were taught to live according to 'dharma'—the path of righteousness—striving to do good, care for others, and seek justice for the vulnerable. My parents, like so many others, instilled in us the importance of kindness, peace, and community.

Yet, amid all these rituals, something was missing. We were told to be good and to live righteously, but no one told me that God loved me personally, that He cared about my everyday life, or that he desired a relationship with me. We had no concept of 'sin' as something deeply embedded in every human heart, separating us from the divine. It wasn't until I encountered the Word of God that I began to understand the root cause of sin and the profound impact it has on our lives and human civilisation.

Here is a summary of insights I have gained from The Holy Bible about human sin and its devastating consequences:

1. Sin as Separation from God

In the Bible, 'sin' is much more than simply doing wrong things. It is a condition—a separation from God. Sin is not just a matter of external actions but the internal reality of our hearts. Sin means that our thoughts, attitudes, and actions are contrary to God's will, and this disrupts our relationship with Him.

In my upbringing, similar to the principles found in Hinduism, there was a strong emphasis on **Dharma**—the importance of living righteously to attain a higher state of spiritual purity. However, what I failed to recognise was that the core issue extended beyond my outward actions; it was deeply rooted in the condition of my heart.

Romans 3:23 reminds us, *For all have sinned and fall short of the glory of God.* This scripture profoundly impacted me, illuminating the universality of sin. It affects everyone, regardless of how good or righteous they may appear on the surface. This realisation was a turning point in my understanding of spirituality and righteousness.

When I reflect on the concept of **Adharma**, or unrighteousness, in Hinduism, I notice a striking parallel. Just as Adharma creates a barrier to spiritual progress, sin creates a chasm between us and our Creator. It's not merely about breaking rules; it's about the deterioration of a relationship.

Adharma is viewed as a force that leads individuals away from their true path, preventing them from achieving their spiritual goals. In much the same way, sin distances us from God, who desires a close and intimate relationship with us. This separation is not just a consequence of our actions but stems from the state of our hearts—hearts that are inclined toward selfishness and disobedience.

Understanding this connection between **Dharma** and **Adharma** with the biblical concept of sin has deepened my appreciation for God's grace. It underscores the importance of inner transformation, not just external compliance.

God's desire is for us to experience true spiritual renewal. As we acknowledge our shortcomings and the distance that sin creates, we open ourselves to His redeeming love. Just as the teachings of Dharma encourage righteousness, the message of Christ calls us to a new life where our hearts can be transformed, enabling us to draw nearer to God.

Ultimately, this journey is about restoration—a return to a loving relationship with our Creator, who offers forgiveness and the gift of a new heart. Through faith in Him, we can overcome the barriers of sin and Adharma, embracing a path that leads to spiritual fulfilment and a deeper connection with God.

As I wrote earlier, God's restoration and reconciliation are beautifully illustrated in 2 Corinthians 5:18-19, which states, *All this is from*

God, who reconciled us to Himself through Christ and gave us the ministry of reconciliation: that God was reconciling the world to Himself in Christ, not counting people's sins against them.

Through His grace, we are offered a chance to be restored to a right relationship with Him, as emphasised in *Psalm 23:3*, 'He restores my soul; He guides me along the right paths for His name's sake.' We are empowered to choose the right path because we are in the right standing with God and grounded in His Word.

2. Sin as Rebellion Against God's Law

The Bible teaches that sin is more than just moral failure—it is a rebellion against God's law. It is a conscious or unconscious choice to go against the moral order God has established for human flourishing. In my traditional upbringing, I was taught that living according to dharma was essential to maintaining balance and order in life, much like how karma operates in Hindu thought.

However, I came to understand that sin in the biblical sense is not merely about actions and consequences—it is about rejecting God's authority over our lives. 1 John 3:4 says, *Everyone who sins breaks the law; in fact, sin is lawlessness.* This struck me deeply because it made me realise that my attempts to live righteously on my own strength were not enough. I was violating God's divine law, not just social norms.

3. Sin as Moral Failure and Missing the Mark

In the Bible, sin is also described as 'missing the mark'. God's standard is holiness, and anything less than that is sin. The Hebrew word for sin, Chata, literally means 'to miss the target'. Growing up, I tried to align my actions with what I thought was righteousness, but no matter how much I tried, I always fell short.

This struggle reminded me of Romans 7:19, which says, *For I do not do the good I want to do, but the evil I do not want to do—this I keep on doing.* This verse perfectly describes my life. Despite my best efforts to live rightly, I realised that sin wasn't just about the actions I committed but about the 'inner corruption' that caused me to miss the mark again and again.

4. **Sin's Consequences:** Separation, Death, and Suffering

The Bible reveals that the ultimate consequence of sin is spiritual death and eternal separation from God. This was something I had not fully understood before. While I was familiar with the Hindu concept of Samsara (the cycle of rebirth) and Moksha (liberation), I learned that sin, from a Christian perspective, is like a moral debt that leads to spiritual death.

Romans 6:23 says, *For the wages of sin is death, but the gift of God is eternal life in Christ Jesus our Lord.* This verse gave me clarity that sin's consequences are far greater than we often realise. While karma teaches that bad actions must be repaid in future lives, the Bible teaches that sin leads to spiritual death. But God, in His mercy, offers eternal life through Jesus Christ. This truth offered me hope—a hope that transcended the endless cycle of karma and rebirth.

5. **Sin as an Internal Condition, Not Just External Actions**

Growing up, I learned the importance of trying to purify my mind and heart, a fundamental pursuit in Hinduism. This often involved a series of rituals, such as lighting a lamp, applying white ash stripes on my forehead and arms, burning incense, and bowing down to various idols and images in our 'gods room'. I felt a sense of fulfilment each time I sincerely completed these acts.

However, when I began reading the teachings of Jesus, I realised that sin starts in the heart. Jesus emphasised that it wasn't just about avoiding bad actions but about confronting the inner desires and intentions that lead to those actions.

In Matthew 5:28, Jesus says, *But I tell you that anyone who looks at a woman lustfully has already committed adultery with her in his heart.* This teaching completely changed my perspective. Jesus made it clear that sin isn't just about what we do on the outside but what we harbour in our hearts—our thoughts, our pride, our anger. The need for inner transformation became clear to me.

6. The Hope of Forgiveness and Redemption

The most beautiful discovery I made was that, despite the weight of sin and its consequences, there is hope. God does not leave us in our broken state. Through Jesus Christ, there is forgiveness, redemption, and reconciliation.

While karma suggests that every action has a corresponding reaction, the Bible offers something radical—grace. 1 John 1:9 says, *If we confess our sins, he is faithful and just and will forgive us our sins and purify us from all unrighteousness.* This was the good news I had been searching for. No longer was I bound by the need to repay every wrong; Jesus had taken my place and offered me forgiveness and freedom.

As you meditate on this, remember that God's grace is always greater than your sin. He stands ready to forgive, to heal, and to restore. Like me, you may have grown up trying to do good but feeling that it's never enough. Let today be the day that you stop trying to earn God's love and start receiving it as the gift that it is.

In Christ, we find freedom from sin and the promise of eternal life. Will you accept His invitation today?

Conclusion

We are all born with a **sinful nature**, inclined toward selfishness and rebellion. This inherent condition separates us from God and disrupts our relationship with Him. As Jeremiah 17:9 says,

> *The heart is deceitful above all things and desperately wicked; who can know it?*

Growing up, I pursued righteousness through cultural traditions and rituals, believing that external acts could bring me closer to God. Yet, these efforts never addressed the deeper issue—the condition of my heart, where sin truly begins.

Through the Bible, I came to understand the true nature of sin. It is more than moral failure; it is rebellion against God, separation from Him, and an inward condition that leads to spiritual death.

As Romans 6:23 explains:

> *For the wages of sin is death, but the gift of God is eternal life in Christ Jesus our Lord.*

No matter how hard I tried to live rightly, I continually fell short. I realised that sin isn't just about external actions—it also includes the **thoughts and intentions of the heart**.

As **Jesus** said in Matthew 5:28:

> *But I say to you that whoever looks at a woman to lust for her has already committed adultery with her in his heart.*

This understanding revealed my desperate need for **redemption** and a **new heart**.

The turning point came when I encountered **God's grace through Jesus Christ**.

Unlike the endless cycle of karma, which is based on personal effort and consequences, Jesus offered **complete forgiveness and reconciliation**. He took the punishment for my sins upon Himself, breaking the cycle of striving and bringing true peace.

As God promises in Ezekiel 36:26:

> *I will give you a new heart and put a new spirit within you.*

He transformed me from within, changing not just my behaviour but my very nature.

This journey has taught me a profound truth: **salvation is not something we can earn; it is a gift we receive by faith**. God's love restores our relationship with Him, and His grace empowers us to live in righteousness and purpose.

Sin no longer defines who I am—His **grace** does.

Today, I encourage you to stop striving to earn God's love. Instead, receive His gift of **forgiveness and renewal** through faith in Jesus Christ.

I have come to understand that **God's Word** acts like a powerful **spiritual mirror**, revealing our true intentions and desires.

As Hebrews 4:12 declares:

> *For the word of God is living and powerful, and sharper than any two-edged sword, piercing even to the division of soul and spirit, and of joints and marrow, and is a discerner of the thoughts and intents of the heart.*

The Word of God not only exposes our outward actions but also uncovers the hidden motives behind them. With **grace and wisdom**, God corrects us, leading us toward **humility**, **repentance**, and **obedience**.

Living the Message: Practical Questions

1. Are there areas in your life where you rely on external actions rather than seeking inner transformation through God's grace?
   _____
   _____
   _____

2. How can you surrender the areas of your heart where sin may still hold power, trusting God for renewal?
   _____
   _____
   _____

3. Have you experienced the freedom of God's forgiveness, and how might His grace change your perspective on life and relationships?
   _____
   _____
   _____

CHAPTER 11

The Power of The Sunrise

![Illustration of a robed figure standing on a path, facing a radiant figure with outstretched arms emerging from a brilliant sunrise over fields and mountains.]

Jesus, The Master Storyteller

Over the past 30 years of studying the Bible, I've discovered profound life lessons—often revealed through its powerful stories. For me, Jesus is the greatest storyteller of all time. As God in human form, He used parables to reveal the heart of the Father, illustrating God's character, love, and truth in ways people could understand.

Many of God's promises and His power are woven into these stories, offering timeless wisdom for those who listen with faith.

In the same spirit, I'd like to share two powerful stories from my own life—testimonies that demonstrate the power of prayer and the transforming joy of worship.

The Joy of the Lord

Our family had an unforgettable experience when we visited **Israel** for the first time a few years ago. While touring **Mount Zion**, near the traditional tomb of **King David**, we witnessed something extraordinary. A group of local Jewish families, along with many young children, were joyfully singing and dancing in the streets. Their exuberance was contagious, and soon, members of our tour group couldn't help but join in their celebration.

As we became immersed in the vibrant music, singing, and dancing—something I had never experienced before—a question stirred in my heart:

What is the source of such overflowing joy? Then I was reminded of the story of **King David**, the great worshiper of God, who danced before the Lord with all his might. **2 Samuel 6:14 (NKJV)** tells us:

> *Then David danced before the Lord with all his might, and David was wearing a linen ephod.*

At that moment, I understood something deeper. The joy we were witnessing wasn't just cultural or traditional—it was a reflection of the **Spirit of God**, alive and present. This joy springs from **worshipping God in spirit and truth**, as Jesus taught in John 4:24

> *God is Spirit, and those who worship Him must worship in spirit and truth.*

This revelation left a profound mark on me. I realised that true joy isn't rooted in circumstances or rituals but in the presence of God Himself. What we experienced on Mount Zion was a **glimpse of God's heart**—His desire to dwell among those who worship Him wholeheartedly. I will never forget that day. It revealed a deep and powerful truth:

The Spirit of God is alive, and His presence brings joy and transformation to all who draw near to Him.

A Powerful Prophetic Word Fulfilled

I believe this second story is worth sharing.

While our group was visiting Ein Karem, the traditional site where Mary, the mother of Jesus, visited her relative Elizabeth (Luke 1:39-40), we experienced a deeply moving moment. Our group leader, Pastor Anil Kant, shared a devotional message from that hilltop, which was being streamed live to viewers overseas.

As Pastor Anil was delivering his message, he paused and began to prophesy over our daughter, Roshni.

He said,

> "Roshni, God is about to do something new in your life. He is going to bring a godly man to be your husband soon. Together, you will share the good news of the Lord in many places."

He then also prophesied a similar blessing over his daughter, Shreya, who was standing beside Roshni.

We were deeply moved and praised God for this incredible word of knowledge. Within a year, this prophecy came to pass. Roshni became engaged and married Joel, a godly man. Now, they are expecting their first child—our first grandchild! Shortly after Roshni's wedding, Shreya was also married.

I was reminded of another prophetic word spoken over Roshni when she was just 14 years old. It declared that God would anoint her to minister to the brokenhearted through **songs of deliverance**—a promise we have seen fulfilled in many ways.

As we reflect on these testimonies, we are reminded of **God's faithfulness**. Just as Mary sang in **Luke 1:46-49**

> *My soul magnifies the Lord, and my spirit has rejoiced in God my Savior. For He who is mighty has done great things for me, and holy is His name.*

We give thanks and praise to God for His **unfailing mercy** and **faithfulness** in our lives.

That moment at **Ein Karem** remains a powerful reminder that God fulfils His promises in ways beyond what we can ask or imagine (Ephesians 3:20).

Later, Pastor Anil prophesied over me as well, saying:

God is giving you a new name, 'Prem-Anand,' which means 'Love and Joy,' symbolizing the first two fruits of the Holy Spirit.

I firmly believe that this book is the fruit of that prophetic word—a testimony I have embraced with all my heart.

Jesus Reveals God's Heart

The Parable of the Prodigal Son is one of Jesus' most well-known stories, found in Luke 15:11-32. It tells of a younger son who demands his inheritance, squanders it in reckless living, and returns home in shame—only to be welcomed by his father with open arms. This powerful story reveals God's unconditional love, forgiveness, and desire to restore those who turn back to Him. Here are the three key points.

1. **Rebellion and Repentance** The son rejects his father's love, seeking happiness through worldly pleasures. After squandering his wealth, he realises the emptiness of his pursuits. This leads to repentance and returning to his father, acknowledging his mistakes and his rebellion.
2. **Forgiveness and Embrace** The father, seeing his son from a distance, runs to embrace him, demonstrating unconditional love and forgiveness. He welcomes his son without scolding, illustrating God's readiness to forgive and restore anyone who turns back to Him.
3. **Restoration** The father restores his son to his rightful place, celebrating with a feast. This shows God's deep desire to redeem, not punish, and for us to experience fulfilled lives in Him.

This story reminds us that all have sinned, as Romans 3:23 reveals our true nature. Without God's love, we cannot truly love ourselves or others. Through accepting God's love and grace, we find fulfilment and extend that love to others.

Like the lost son, I realised my need for God's mercy. In repentance, I discovered a transformative love that changed me to know God better. The Bible invites us to embrace this journey, returning to the loving arms of our Father.

John 1:1-18 unveils **the Word of God**, the divine **Logos**—God's ultimate expression of wisdom, power, and purpose. From the beginning, as written in Genesis 1 and 2, God spoke creation into existence, shaping the world with His intentional design. I now understand with awe and clarity that **we were created for His eternal pleasure.** This truth is not just profound—it is breathtaking.

But let me ask you: **How do you express love for someone you long to spend eternity with?**

Consider the Taj Mahal—a timeless masterpiece, built by a king to immortalise his love for his wife. He wanted the world to witness the depth of his devotion.

When I first saw it, I was captivated by its grandeur. But then a thought struck me: If an earthly king could go to such lengths for love, **how much greater must the love of the God of the universe be?**

And John 15:13 reveals the answer:

> *Greater love has no one than this: to lay down one's life*
> *for one's friends.*

God has indeed revealed His love, not through marble or stone but through the ultimate sacrifice of Jesus Christ. While the Taj Mahal is a monument to love that can be admired from afar, the cross of Christ is an act of love that embraces us up close. It is not built with marble and jewels but with the very blood of God's Son.

The call of the cross is an invitation into an eternal relationship with Him - He is the God of the universe!

His love is not carved in stone—it is written on the cross. And the cross expresses a divine exchange to make us right with God. I have been learning to taste His love and goodness every day.

The Holy Bible: 66 Books with One Message!

When I was growing up, no one ever shared with me the most essential message of God. To me, God was an unfathomable being, and no one seemed to have the right words to convey His true nature. Allow me to introduce you to the Holy Bible; this book provides a unique opportunity to delve into the profound depth and richness of its message.

The most important message of the Holy Bible is this:

- God loves you.
- But your sins have separated you from His love.
- But God invites you to a personal relationship through Jesus.
- And He is waiting to reveal Himself to you as your Creator and Redeemer.

John 3:16 demonstrates this powerful message:

> *For God so loved the world that He gave His one and only Son, that whoever believes in Him shall not perish but have eternal life.*

This verse illustrates God's immense love and desire for all to come to Him through faith in Jesus.

The Bible is a collection of 66 books written by over 40 authors across a span of more than 2,000 years, yet it presents a singular, cohesive revelation of God. At its core, the Bible reveals God as the Creator and Sustainer of the universe, who intricately designs and upholds all of creation. He is depicted as the Provider who meets our needs, the Healer who restores our bodies and souls, and the Miracle Worker who intervenes in our lives in extraordinary ways.

Throughout the Scriptures, God is shown as a Forgiver, offering grace and redemption to those who seek Him. He is the Lover who longs for a relationship with humanity, a Father who cares for His children, and the Lamb of God who sacrificed Himself for our salvation. The Bible describes Him as a Refining Fire, purifying us through trials and challenges, and as the Beginning and the End, embodying the eternal nature of existence.

Moreover, God is proclaimed as the King of Kings and Lord of Lords, a figure of ultimate authority who reigns over all. His character is trustworthy and true, represented as the Almighty, the True Vine, and the Lover of our souls.

What makes the Bible truly remarkable is the precise fulfilment of its prophetic words throughout human history. Each prophecy, ranging from the coming of the Messiah to the events of the early church, has unfolded as foretold, providing a testament to the reliability and divine inspiration of the Scriptures.

As you explore the Bible, you will discover a narrative that invites you into a deep and personal relationship with this incredible God, one who desires to reveal Himself fully to all who seek Him. Through its pages, you will find answers to life's profound questions and an invitation to experience the fullness of His love and grace.

Love in Action is Compassion

I discovered that love is not merely a feeling; it is a person—Jesus, who embodies compassion and practical help. Many have attempted to define love, including famous authors like Shakespeare, but none come close to the perfect demonstration of love found in Jesus' life and sacrifice. His actions illustrate the depth of God's love, as captured in the grace I have experienced. Songs like 'Amazing Grace' continue to comfort countless souls, revealing the transformative power of God's love.

God's Inviting Message: I Love You

The Bible consistently conveys a powerful and unified message: **"I love you."** Through its remarkable verses, we see God's love, mercy, compassion, kindness, wisdom, and judgment inviting fallen humanity into a relationship with Him. But why do most people find it hard to believe this truth? To answer that, we need to look at the Word of God.

The Cosmic War Between Two Kingdoms

The Bible reveals that we are caught up in a war between two kingdoms: the Kingdom of God, belonging to the Creator of Heaven and Earth, and the Kingdom of the devil, also known as Satan, the deceiver and accuser. He reigns as the king of his dark kingdom, accompanied by countless evil spirits who serve his purpose of opposing God and His people.

Satan was originally Lucifer, an archangel who was cast out of heaven due to his pride and rebellion against God.

Isaiah 14:12-15 captures this story of rebellion.

> *How you have fallen from heaven, O Lucifer, son of the morning! How you are cut down to the ground, you who weakened the nations! For you have said in your heart 'I will ascend into heaven, I will exalt my throne above the stars of God; I will sit on the mount of the congregation on the farthest sides of the north; I will ascend above the heights of the clouds, I will be like the Most High. Yet you shall be brought down to Sheol, to the lowest depths of the Pit.*

Similarly, Ezekiel 28:17 speaks of satan's pride.

Your heart was lifted because of your beauty; you corrupted your wisdom for the sake of your splendour. I cast you to the ground, I laid you before kings, that they might gaze at you. This passage illustrates the tragic downfall of Satan and the establishment of the battle between good and evil.

The struggle of humanity began with the cunning deception of Adam and Eve by Satan, as recorded in Genesis 3:1-6. Their choice to disobey God led to the entrance of sin into the world.

However, the story doesn't end there. From the very moment of humanity's fall, the Bible also promises restoration. In Genesis 3:15, God foreshadows victory over sin and Satan. *And I will put enmity between you and the woman, and between your offspring and hers; he will crush your head, and you will strike his heel.* This overarching narrative underscores the hope and grace offered to fallen humanity through Christ, inviting us to choose the Kingdom of God and experience His love and restoration.

The Promises of The Sunrise

From the beginning, God promised redemption. After the fall of Adam and Eve, He declared that one day the offspring of the woman would crush the head of the serpent (Genesis 3:15). This was the first glimpse of His plan to redeem humanity—bringing us out of the kingdom of darkness and into the Kingdom of Light through Jesus Christ.

Throughout history, humanity has longed for deliverance from darkness, confusion, and death. This universal desire is reflected even in ancient Indian Vedic texts:

> Asato ma sadgamaya,
> Tamaso ma jyotirgamaya,
> Mrityor ma amritam gamaya.
> Om Shaantih Shaantih Shaantih.

Which translates to:

> Lead us from the unreal to the real,
> From darkness to light,
> From death to immortality.
> Aum peace, peace, peace!

This ancient prayer expresses a deep human longing for truth, light, and eternal life. The **Bible** reveals that this longing finds its **true fulfilment** in **Jesus Christ**, who said:

> *I am the light of the world. Whoever follows me will never walk in darkness, but will have the light of life.* (John 8:12)

Jesus not only proclaimed to be the **light**, but He also conquered **sin and death** through His resurrection. As **Romans 6:9** declares:

> *Knowing that Christ, having been raised from the dead, dies no more. Death no longer has dominion over Him.*

Through faith in **Jesus,** we are offered **eternal life,** freedom from the darkness of sin, and reconciliation with **God the Father.** He is the fulfilment of humanity's deepest cry for salvation—the true and living **Light of the World.**

Seven Verses That Summarise God's Heart

Consider these seven significant verses that summarise the heart of God. Let the Sunrise of Lord Jesus lead you into your true identity as the child of God:

1. **John 3:16**

   For God so loved the world that He gave His one and only Son, that whoever believes in Him shall not perish but have eternal life.

2. **Matthew 11:28-30**

   Come to me, all you who are weary and burdened, and I will give you rest. Take my yoke upon you and learn from me, for I am gentle and humble in heart, and you will find rest for your souls.

3. **Romans 10:13**

   For everyone who calls on the name of the Lord will be saved.

4. **Revelation 3:20**

   Here I am! I stand at the door and knock. If anyone hears my voice and opens the door, I will come in and eat with that person, and they will be with me.

5. **Isaiah 1:18**

   Come now, let us settle the matter, says the Lord. Though your sins are like scarlet, they shall be as white as snow; though they are red as crimson, they shall be like wool.

6. **Jeremiah 29:11**

   For I know the plans I have for you, declares the Lord, plans to prosper you and not to harm you, plans to give you hope and a future.

7. **Psalm 119:105**

   Your word is a lamp for my feet, a light on my path.

Modern Miracle of God

I firmly believe that the **rebirth of Israel as a nation in 1948**, after nearly 2,000 years of dispersion, is one of the most remarkable and **breathtaking fulfillments of biblical prophecy** in modern times. No other nation in history has been scattered for so long and yet restored to its ancient homeland with its language, culture, and identity intact.

This divine and decisive event could only have been accomplished by the **supernatural power and faithfulness of God**. Israel's restoration is a powerful reminder that God's Word is true, and He remains faithful to His covenant promises.

Here are **seven reasons,** supported by Scripture, why Israel stands today as a **living testimony of God's miraculous work and faithfulness:**

1. **The Fulfillment of Prophecy** - Isaiah 66:8

   Who has ever heard of such things? Who has ever seen things like this? Can a country be born in a day or a nation be brought forth in a moment? Yet no sooner is Zion in labour than she gives birth to her children.

2. **God's Everlasting Covenant** - Genesis 17:7-8

   I will establish my covenant as an everlasting covenant between me and you and your descendants after you for the generations to come, to be your God and the God of your descendants after you. The whole land of Canaan, where you now reside as a foreigner, I will give as an everlasting possession to you and your descendants after you, and I will be their God.

Israel's existence today testifies to God's unbroken covenant with Abraham and his descendants.

3. **The Restoration of the Land** - Ezekiel 36:34-35

   The desolate land will be cultivated instead of lying desolate in the sight of all who pass through it. They will say, 'This land that was laid waste has become like the garden of Eden; the cities that were lying in ruins, desolate and destroyed, are now fortified and inhabited.

The transformation of Israel's barren land into a thriving agricultural hub fulfils God's promises of restoration.

4. **The Ingathering of Exiles** - Isaiah 43:5-6

> *Do not be afraid, for I am with you; I will bring your children from the east and gather you from the west. I will say to the north, 'Give them up!' and to the south, 'Do not hold them back.' Bring my sons from afar and my daughters from the ends of the earth.*

The return of Jews from around the world to their ancestral homeland is a visible miracle of God's promise.

5. **A Light to the Nations** - *Isaiah 49:6*

> *I will also make you a light for the Gentiles, that my salvation may reach the ends of the earth.*

Israel's technological, medical, and spiritual contributions continue to impact the world, fulfilling its role as a light to the nations.

6. **The Preservation of the People** - Jeremiah 31:35-36

> *This is what the Lord says, he who appoints the sun to shine by day, who decrees the moon and stars to shine by night, who stirs up the sea so that its waves roar—the Lord Almighty is his name: 'Only if these decrees vanish from my sight,' declares the Lord, 'will Israel ever cease being a nation before me.'*

Despite countless attempts to destroy them, the Jewish people have endured, demonstrating God's faithfulness.

7. **The Central Role in God's Plan** - Zechariah 2:12

The Lord will inherit Judah as his portion in the holy land and will again choose Jerusalem.

Jerusalem remains central to God's redemptive plan, reminding us of His eternal purposes.

These seven points and Scriptures illustrate that Israel's existence, restoration, and impact are undeniable evidence of a loving God who fulfils His promises.

Conclusion: The Supernatural Book

I firmly believe that the Bible is unlike any other book—it is a Supernatural Book, divinely inspired, prophetically accurate, and profoundly transformative. Through its pages of faith, I have personally experienced its life-changing power.

Romans 10:17 states, *So faith comes from hearing, and hearing through the word of Christ.* This verse reminds me that spiritual growth comes from immersing ourselves in God's Word.

I have discovered that the Bible offers practical guidance, answers life's deepest questions, and invites us into a personal relationship with God. It reveals His unchanging love through timeless wisdom and transformative power, providing hope, redemption, and a purpose-filled life to all who seek Him.

I encourage you to put this truth to the test by applying it to the challenges in your own life. See how these ancient truths can guide you toward a purpose-driven life, just as Jesus promised in John 10:10: *I have come that they may have life, and have it to the full.*

Two leaders who have reached convincing conclusions about the Holy Bible:

Mahatma Gandhi
You Christians look after a document containing enough dynamite to blow all civilisation to pieces, turn the world upside down, and bring peace to a battle-torn planet.

George Washington
It is impossible to rightly govern a nation without God and the Bible.

Living the Message: Practical Questions

1. How does the story of the Prodigal Son challenge your understanding of God's forgiveness and love?

   _____
   _____
   _____

2. What aspects of your life reflect self-reliance, and how can you surrender them to God's grace?

   _____
   _____
   _____

3. How might applying the teachings of the Bible address struggles like fear, pride, or a lack of purpose in your life?

   _____
   _____
   _____

CHAPTER 12

The Eternal Sunrise

"But for you ou who wo fear His name, the sun of will righteousness with healing with healing arises healing In His wings." Malachi 4:2

In My Father's house are many mansions; if it were not so, I would have told you. I am going to prepare a place for you. John 14:2

Dear friend, Heaven is real!

When I sought God about Heaven, I earnestly asked, "We know that eternity is forever and ever, so what will we be doing in Heaven apart from singing and worshipping You?"

The answer I received from God took my breath away. In my spirit, I heard a gentle whisper: "Forever and ever, you will be discovering My goodness and mercy." This profound response brings Psalm 23:6 to life.

> *Surely your goodness and love will follow me all the days of my life, and I will dwell in the house of the Lord forever.*

Before I came to faith in Jesus, Heaven felt like a mythical place, and I struggled to comprehend the concept of eternity. Much of my upbringing emphasised the importance of trying to be a good person, with the hope that this would somehow earn me a ticket to Heaven. However, the Bible clearly states that our good works cannot secure a place in paradise. Ephesians 2:8-9 affirms this truth:

> *For it is by grace you have been saved, through faith—and this is not from yourselves, it is the gift of God—not by works so that no one can boast.*

Heaven is not earned; it is a gift for those who trust in the blood of Jesus and His death and resurrection. This realisation transformed my understanding of salvation and the true path to eternal life.

Many books and songs have been written to joke about and belittle the realities of Heaven and Hell. However, the Bible speaks with full authority and truth regarding these two realities. Therefore, I do not entertain jokes or discussions that tend to downplay the Word of God. The mindset of many people has been corrupted by such deep deception. As Scripture reminds us in John 8:32, *Then you will know the truth, and the truth will set you free.*

I pray that they will come to know this truth, which can liberate them from the dangerous errors surrounding these important subjects.

For me, Heaven isn't just a comforting idea or wishful thinking—it's a **real invitation from God.** He desires a personal relationship with me, offering **forgiveness, restoration**, and the promise of **eternal life** through Jesus Christ. (John 3:16)

We were created for eternity. As Ecclesiastes 3:11 says, *He (God) has also set eternity in the human heart.* Deep within every person is an awareness that this life is not all there is.

This Is Undeniable—Heaven Is Our Real Home!

Here are five powerful Bible verses that boldly affirm the promise and reality of Heaven:

1. **John 14:2-3**

   My Father's house has many rooms; if that were not so, would I have told you that I am going there to prepare a place for you? And if I go and prepare a place for you, I will come back and take you to be with me so that you also may be where I am.

This verse assures us that Heaven is a prepared place for believers, emphasising Jesus' promise of eternal fellowship with Him.

2. **Philippians 3:20**

   But our citizenship is in heaven. And we eagerly await a Saviour from there, the Lord Jesus Christ.

This verse reminds us that, as believers, our true home is in Heaven, and we can look forward to the return of Christ.

3. **Revelation 21:1-4**

   Then I saw a new heaven and a new earth, for the first heaven and the first earth had passed away, and there was no longer any sea. I saw the Holy City, the new Jerusalem, coming down out of heaven from God, prepared as a bride beautifully dressed for her husband. And I heard a loud voice from the throne saying, 'Look! God's dwelling place is now among the people, and he will dwell with them. They will be his people, and God himself will be with them and be their God. He will wipe every tear from their eye. There will be no more death...

This passage offers a vivid description of the new Heaven and new Earth, emphasising God's presence and the restoration of all things.

4. **Matthew 5:12**

   Rejoice and be glad, because great is your reward in heaven, for in the same way they persecuted the prophets who were before you.

Jesus encourages believers to find joy in their struggles, as they have a great reward waiting for them in Heaven.

5. **2 Corinthians 5:1**

   For we know that if the earthly tent we live in is destroyed, we have a building from God, an eternal house in heaven, not built by human hands.

This verse reassures us of the eternal dwelling that awaits believers in Heaven, contrasting our temporary earthly existence with the permanence of God's promises.

These verses collectively affirm the reality of Heaven, highlighting it as a place of hope, restoration, and eternal fellowship with God.

My Parents' Journey to Eternal Peace

Before my parents entered eternity, they experienced the joy of reconciliation with God. The Bible reminds us that *all have sinned and fallen short of God's glory* in Romans 3:23, but through Yeshua, God offers restoration. One of my life's greatest blessings was sharing the Gospel with my parents, leading them to this precious reconciliation.

After encountering God supernaturally, I prayed fervently for my parents' salvation. Unsure how to communicate the Good News, I sought wisdom from the Lord, who inspired me to share my testimony in a heartfelt letter written in Kannada, our native language. Though I hadn't used the language in years, I prayed for clarity and began writing late one night. By morning, I had penned over ten pages with a joy that only God could provide.

I recounted how God had guided and protected me from my childhood struggles to my life-changing encounter with Him. I emphasised the truth of Ephesians 2:8-9: Salvation is a gift of grace through faith in Yeshua, not through works. God's faithfulness was evident as He worked in my parents' hearts, bringing them peace and redemption. Their journey reminded me of God's greater story of love, grace, and reconciliation.

The Eternal Sunrise is Real

The concept of an 'Eternal Sunrise' symbolises the everlasting light, hope, and new beginnings found in God's presence. While the term 'Eternal Sunrise' is not explicitly used in the Bible, many verses allude to the idea of God's eternal light and the promise of a new dawn in His kingdom.

Here are several key scriptures related to the theme of eternal light, hope, and renewal that can be connected to the truth about 'The Eternal Sunrise':

1. **Revelation 22:5**

   There will be no more night. They will not need the light of a lamp or the light of the sun, for the Lord God will give them light. And they will reign forever and ever.

This verse speaks of the eternal light that comes from God, which eliminates all darkness, much like an eternal sunrise that never fades.

2. **Isaiah 60:19-20**

   The sun will no more be your light by day, nor will the brightness of the moon shine on you, for the Lord will be your everlasting light, and your God will be your glory. Your sun will never set again, and your moon will wane no more; the Lord will be your everlasting light, and your days of sorrow will end.

This beautiful prophecy describes a future where God Himself is the eternal light, much like an eternal sunrise that brings never-ending hope and joy.

3. **Psalm 112:4**

   Even in darkness, light dawns for the upright, for those who are gracious and compassionate and righteous.

Here, light is metaphorically tied to God's continued blessing and guidance, reminiscent of an eternal dawn for those who walk in righteousness.

4. **Malachi 4:2**

   But for you who revere my name, the sun of righteousness will rise with healing in its rays. And you will go out and frolic like well-fed calves.

This verse directly connects the rising sun with righteousness and healing, a promise of God's eternal care and restoration.

THE ETERNAL SUNRISE

5. **Luke 1:78-79**

   Because of the tender mercy of our God, by which the rising sun will come to us from heaven to shine on those living in darkness and the shadow of death, to guide our feet into the path of peace.

The rising sun here is a metaphor for the coming of Jesus, offering eternal light and peace, much like an eternal sunrise that never fades.

6. **Proverbs 4:18**

   The path of the righteous is like the morning sun, shining ever brighter till the full light of day.

This verse speaks of the growing light in the life of the righteous, which can be linked to the idea of an eternal sunrise that continuously grows in brightness.

7. **John 8:12**

   When Jesus spoke again to the people, he said, 'I am the light of the world. Whoever follows me will never walk in darkness but will have the light of life.

Jesus' promise to be the light of life reflects the concept of an eternal source of light and life, akin to an everlasting sunrise.

8. **Psalm 30:5**

    For his anger lasts only a moment, but his favour lasts a lifetime; weeping may stay for the night, but rejoicing comes in the morning.

This verse connects the arrival of morning with joy, symbolising the hope of an eternal dawn that dispels sorrow.

9. **2 Peter 1:19**

    We also have the prophetic message as something completely reliable, and you will do well to pay attention to it, as to a light shining in a dark place, until the day dawns and the morning star rises in your hearts.

The imagery of the morning star rising ties in with the idea of eternal light, a reflection of God's guidance and His kingdom's everlasting hope.

10. **Isaiah 9:2**

    The people walking in darkness have seen a great light; on those living in the land of deep darkness, a light has dawned.

This verse is often associated with the coming of Jesus, the light of the world, bringing hope and salvation, much like an eternal sunrise that breaks the power of darkness.

These scriptures offer a powerful connection between God's eternal presence, the hope of His promises, and the imagery of light, which can be likened to an eternal sunrise that brings everlasting life, peace, and joy.

It was only through the **revelation of the Scriptures** that I began to truly understand the **complete nature of a human being**.

1 Thessalonians 5:23 says:

> *Now may the God of peace Himself sanctify you completely; and may your whole spirit, soul, and body be preserved blameless at the coming of our Lord Jesus Christ.*

This verse teaches that we are made up of **three distinct parts**:

- **Spirit** (*pneuma* in Greek / *ruach* in Hebrew / ātman in Sanskrit)
- **Soul** (*psyche* in Greek/*nephesh* in Hebrew / *jīva* or *manas* in Sanskrit)
- **Body** (*soma* in Greek / *basar* in Hebrew / śarīra in Sanskrit)

Understanding this truth helped me see how God designed us to relate to Him in **spirit**, to ourselves and others through our **soul** (mind, emotions, and will), and to the world through our **body**.

Be certain!

This is the complete design of every human being—clearly revealed in the Holy Scriptures alone and echoed across ancient languages. Understanding this truth transforms how we see ourselves and our relationship with God.

As I conclude this final chapter, I pray and trust that you will 'Find Your Sunrise'. This metaphor represents discovering your true identity and purpose through The Spirit and the Word of God, your Creator. You are loved and highly valued by your Maker. Psalm 19 teaches us that Heaven proclaims this truth.

Just as I cried out to God in my distress and darkness, you, too, can make a bold move toward your own 'Sunrise'. Like me, take a moment to gaze at the night sky and reflect on the following verses from Scripture:

Psalm 19:1-5

> *The heavens declare the glory of God;*
> *The skies proclaim the work of His hands.*
> *Day after day, they pour forth speech;*
> *night after night, they reveal knowledge.*
> *They have no speech; they use no words;*
> *No sound is heard from them.*
> *Yet their voice goes out into all the earth,*
> *their words to the ends of the world.*
> *In the heavens, He has pitched a tent for the sun,*
> *Next time you gaze at the night sky, let your spirit be*
> *open to the messages it carries from above.*

Next time you gaze at the night sky, let your spirit be open to the messages it carries from above.

These verses powerfully convey how creation communicates the glory and greatness of God, highlighting the profound connection between the natural world and divine revelation.

Word of God declares that the heavens and skies proclaim God's glory and creativity, silently revealing His greatness to the ends of the earth. Through creation, God's handiwork speaks without words, testifying to His majesty and eternal power. **Prepare your heart for Your Sunrise.**

In the light of my 'Sunrise' story and God's eternal love, now I invite you to sincerely prepare your heart to receive the greatest gift of life. An Eternal Sunrise Salvation in Jesus' name.

Jeremiah 29:13 states, *You will seek Me and find Me when you search for Me with all your heart.*

This verse emphasises the importance of wholeheartedly seeking God, assuring us that He is ready to be found by those who earnestly pursue Him. This truth also highlights the promise that God is accessible to those who earnestly desire a relationship with Him. Here's a simple yet powerful prayer to start building that relationship today.

Eternal Sunrise Prayer: Salvation (Moksha)

Dear Father God,

I come to You today recognising that I have sinned and fallen short of Your glory. I acknowledge that I need Your grace and forgiveness. Thank you for sending Jesus to be my Savior. I believe in my heart that He died for my sins and rose again, conquering darkness and offering me new life.

I repent of my sins and turn away from my past. I renounce the things that separate me from You. I invite Your light into my life and ask for Your help to live according to Your will.

I receive Your gift of salvation by faith. I confess with my mouth that Jesus is Lord, and I ask You to restore and reconcile me to You. I receive Jesus, the eternal sunrise in my soul.

Thank you for Your incredible love and for giving me a fresh start. I trust in Your promises and choose to follow You from this day forward.

In Jesus' name, I pray. Amen.

Praise The Lord!

Congratulations on your bold and sincere prayer!

Welcome to the family of God.

The Bible assures us in 2 Corinthians 5:17

> *If anyone is in Christ, the new creation has come. The old has gone, the new is here.*

You are now a new creation in Christ, filled with His love and purpose. We encourage you to find a local Bible-based church where you can grow in your faith as a true disciple of Jesus. If you need assistance, feel free to reach out to us. Together, we can help guide you and others toward the 'Eternal Sunrise'.

Here are five essential tips for a new believer to become grounded in the Bible and seek baptism in water and the Holy Spirit:

1. **Establish a regular Bible reading habit**
    Start with the New Testament, focusing on the Gospels (Matthew, Mark, Luke, and John) to understand the life and teachings of Jesus. Set aside dedicated time each day for reading and reflection. Consider using a study Bible or devotional to enhance your understanding.

2. **Join a Bible Study Group or Church Community**
   Connect with other believers by joining a Bible study group or attending a local church. Being part of a community will provide support, encouragement, and opportunities to discuss Scripture and grow together in faith. It's also a great way to learn about baptism and the Holy Spirit.

3. **Seek Baptism in water**
   Water baptism is an important step in your faith journey, symbolising your commitment to follow Christ. Talk to your pastor or church leaders about how to prepare for baptism and understand its significance as an outward expression of your inward faith.

4. **Pray for the Holy Spirit**
   Actively seek the Holy Spirit in your life through prayer. Ask God to fill you with His Spirit, guiding you in your daily walk. Understanding the role of the Holy Spirit is crucial, as He empowers, teaches, and comforts us. Luke 11:13 reminds us that God gives the Holy Spirit to those who ask.

5. **Apply God's Word to your life**
   As you study the Bible, look for ways to apply its teachings to your daily life. This can involve practising love, kindness, and forgiveness, as well as sharing your faith with others. Living out the principles of Scripture will deepen your relationship with God and strengthen your faith.

By following these tips, you can build a strong foundation in your faith, deepen your understanding of God's Word, and actively seek baptism and the work of the Holy Spirit in your life.

Conclusion

Before coming to faith in Jesus, Heaven felt like a distant, mythical concept. Growing up, I believed being a good person would earn me a place in paradise, but the Bible revealed that salvation is a gift of grace, not works (Ephesians 2:8-9). Heaven is real, prepared for believers who trust in Jesus' death and resurrection, as affirmed in John 14:2-3. This understanding transformed my life and assured me of eternal fellowship with God.

The Bible also contrasts Heaven with the reality of Hell, underscoring the eternal consequences of our choices. As John 8:32 reminds us, *You shall know the Truth (Yeshua) and The Truth (Yeshua) will set you free.*

Understanding these truths motivated me to share the Good News with others, including my parents. Through prayer and guidance from God, I shared my testimony with them in a heartfelt letter, leading to their reconciliation with God before their passing. Witnessing their salvation affirmed that God's love extends to all who seek Him.

The concept of an 'Eternal Sunrise' symbolises God's eternal light, hope, and new beginnings. Scriptures such as Revelation 22:5 and Isaiah 60:19-20 speak of a future where God's presence eliminates all darkness, offering eternal joy and peace. This eternal light invites us to a life transformed by grace, anchored in the promise of salvation.

Now, I encourage others to seek their 'Sunrise' by accepting Jesus and experiencing the hope of Heaven. Through prayer, Bible study, and fellowship, new believers can grow in their faith and live out God's purpose.

The journey to the Eternal Sunrise begins with seeking God wholeheartedly (*Jeremiah 29:13*), embracing His gift of salvation, and walking in the light of His love.

Arise and Shine

Once we establish a genuine relationship with God, His light becomes our daily sunrise. We are called to illuminate the world with His love and grace and to serve as effective witnesses to His gospel—the good news.

Below are three simple and effective steps to bring your sunrise into the dark corners of our world. Empowered by His Holy Spirit, we embark on this exciting journey, and as Acts 1:8 reminds us, we become effective witnesses and co-workers in God's marvellous ministry.

1. **Live Out Your Faith**

    Matthew 5:16 - *Let your light shine before others, that they may see your good deeds and glorify your Father in heaven.*

Inspiration: Let your actions reflect God's love. Simple acts of kindness, integrity, and compassion can ignite hope and lead others to seek the source of your light.

2. **Embrace Modern Mindset and Technology**

    1 Corinthians 9:22 - *I have become all things to all people so that by all possible means I might save some.*

If certain foods or meats offend people from other cultures, among whom you live, seek God's guidance and be willing to refrain from them to help lead others to Christ.

For example, eating beef is considered offensive and a barrier to faith for many Indians. I challenge true believers to follow Paul's example:

> 1 Corinthians 9:22-23 - *I've become just about every sort of servant there is in my attempts to lead those I meet into a God-saved life. I did all this because of the Message. I didn't just want to talk about it; I wanted to be in on it! (The Message)*

This passage highlights the Apostle Paul's commitment to adapting his approach to reach diverse groups with the gospel, emphasising his dedication to actively participating in the transformative work of the Message.

Historically, Cross-cultural ministers like **Robert de Nobili** in 17th-century India adapted their dietary practices, including abstaining from beef, to respect Hindu cultural sensitivities and remove barriers to evangelism.

Inspiration: Utilise social media, blogs, podcasts, and videos to share God's message in a way that addresses today's challenges. Create content that bridges ancient truths with modern life, offering practical solutions grounded in godly wisdom.

3. Build Genuine Relationships

> Colossians 4:6 - *Let your conversation be always full of grace, seasoned with salt, so that you may know how to answer everyone.*

Can the Bible message and its purpose be summarised in a short statement?

Answer is yes!

I believe the following statement and an easy-to-understand flow chart are the answer.

The Bible is God's love letter and life guide, revealing His plan to rescue, redeem, and restore every person who chooses to trust in Jesus Christ (John 14:6; Romans 5:8; 1 Peter 3:18)—offering a path to grace, hope, and a new beginning (Luke 15:11-32; Isaiah 35:7).

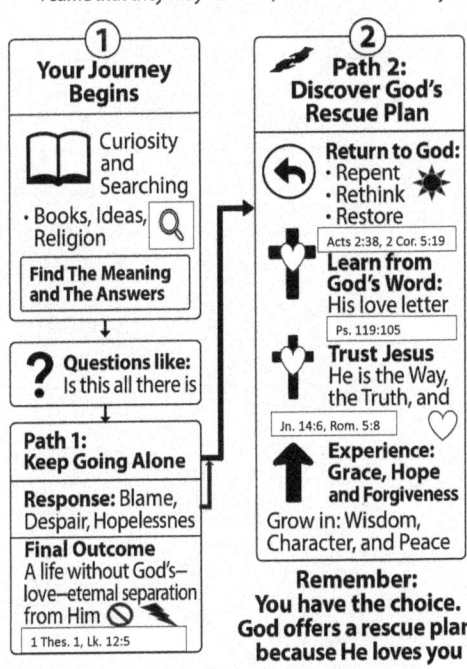

Living the Message: Practical Questions

1. What misconceptions about Heaven or salvation might you need to reevaluate in light of God's grace?
   _____
   _____
   _____

2. How can you actively share the message of God's love and salvation with those closest to you?
   _____
   _____
   _____

3. What steps can you take today to grow in your faith and prepare for the "Eternal Sunrise" of God's eternal promises?
   _____
   _____
   _____

THE ETERNAL SUNRISE

Allow these seven timeless quotes to inspire your reflection on the nature and promises of Heaven.

C.S. Lewis: "Joy is the serious business of Heaven."

Billy Graham: "My home is in Heaven. I'm just travelling through this world."

Jonathan Edwards: "To go to heaven, fully to enjoy God, is infinitely better than the most pleasant accommodations here."

Charles Spurgeon: "There are no crown-wearers in heaven who were not cross-bearers here below."

Rick Warren: "The way you store up treasure in Heaven is by investing in getting people there."

Thomas Moore: "Earth has no sorrow that Heaven cannot heal."

Victor Hugo: "Son, brother, father, lover, friend. There is room in the heart for all the affections, as there is room in heaven for all the stars."

Threads of Love: Our Family Legacy in Photos

Children's children are a crown to the aged, and parents are the pride of their children.
Proverbs 17:6

This timeless photograph, taken over 50 years ago, captures the foundation of our family legacy. My parents, standing as pillars of love and wisdom, are surrounded by my six older siblings and me—the 'Sunrise Baby' at the centre. Each sibling's expression reflects childhood innocence, while the simplicity of that era shaped values that united us. This cherished image evokes warmth, laughter, and the enduring strength of family bonds. Though decades have passed, it remains a vivid testament to our origins and the promise of love that continues to guide us today.

A Glimpse into the Past: Legacy Captured in Time

This cherished 1925 family photo shows my father as a one-year-old, cradled between my grandfather and mother. A fleeting yet profound moment, it holds deep meaning, as my grandfather passed away soon after. Though I never met him, this image offers a glimpse into our family's history and the love surrounding my father. Their faces reflect hope and dreams for the future. This photo connects me to my roots, serving as a bridge to the past and a reminder of the legacy that shapes us today.

> *A good person leaves an inheritance for their children's children.* Proverbs 13:22

A father to the fatherless, a defender of widows, is God in his holy dwelling. *Psalm 68:5*

This poignant photograph captures my two-year-old father and his widowed mother, embodying love and resilience amidst profound loss. Her sorrowful eyes reveal the weight of her husband's absence, yet her determination to protect and nurture her son shines through. Despite the challenges of single motherhood, her unwavering love forged a bond of hope and strength. My father's innocent gaze symbolises the brighter future she strove to provide. This image tells a timeless story of sacrifice, resilience, and enduring love, reminding me of my grandmother's courage and the legacy of devotion that continues to shape our family today.

> *Do not fear, for I am with you; do not be dismayed, for I am your God. I will strengthen you and help you; I will uphold you with my righteous right hand.* Isaiah 41:10

Our family legacy: Our great-grandmother was born around the 1870s. This reminds a promise verse: *His faithfulness continues through all generations. Psalm. 100:5b*

You knit me together...

As I look at my baby photo, a 10-month-old me beaming with joy, I'm reminded of the profound truth in Psalm 139:14 *I praise you because I am fearfully and wonderfully made...*

This image captures the innocence, wonder, and exuberance of life's beginnings, reflecting God's intricate design and purpose. Each smile tells a story of love and care that surrounded me from birth, a testament to His artistry. This photo evokes gratitude for a life woven with intention and guided by His faithfulness. It reminds me that God's love never fails, and every life is a cherished masterpiece in His hands.

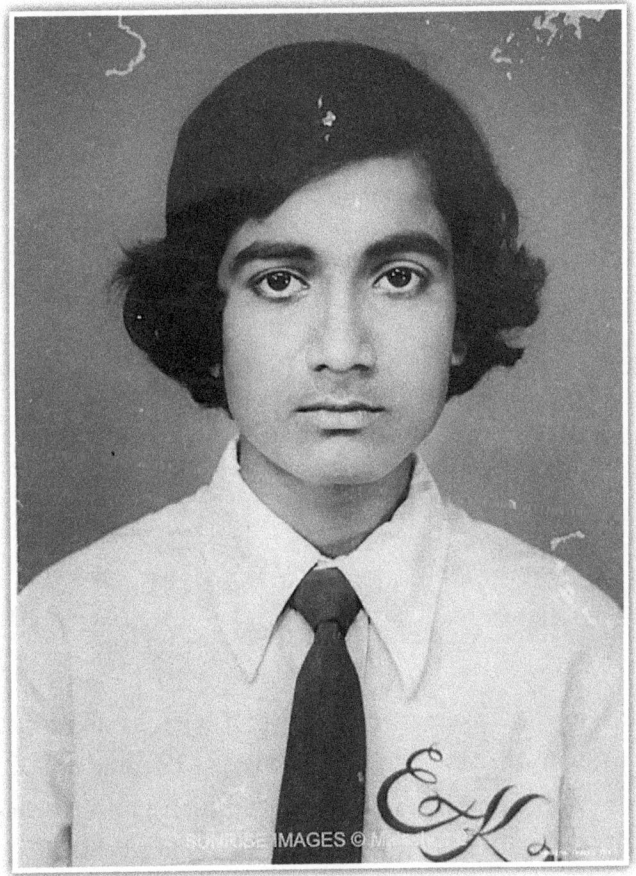

This photo of me as the School Sports Captain at the age of 13 brings back wonderful memories of fun times. I often dreamed of the games and imagined making it to the national team one day. But now, I realise I am part of the greatest team ever—the Lord's Team.

As 1 Corinthians 9:25 reminds us, *Everyone who competes in the games goes into strict training. They do it to get a crown that will not last, but we do it to get a crown that will last forever.*

I visited my birthplace after many years, and as I walked through its familiar paths, memories of my childhood came flooding back. I recalled encounters with scorpions and other vivid moments that shaped my early years. As I reflected, my heart was overwhelmed with gratitude for God's faithfulness through it all.

I began to hear the echoes of joy and laughter from those days. I remembered the starry nights filled with stories my mother shared, the playful fights with my siblings, and the festive noise that filled the air. Even the taste of sweets seemed to linger in my soul, bringing a warm sense of nostalgia and blessing.

> *I remember the days of old; I meditate on all your works and consider what your hands have done.* Psalm 143:5

THE ETERNAL SUNRISE

This photo is with our neurologist—the one who identified the issues with my wife's spinal cord during her pregnancy. He urgently arranged an emergency MRI, which led to a life-saving laminectomy, ultimately saving **two lives**. This was the first time he met our miracle baby, **Roshni**, whose life was part of that incredible story. Two lives saved—one miracle story.

> *"Before I formed you in the womb I knew you, before you were born I set you apart."* – Jeremiah 1:5

In this powerful and prophetic photo from 2017, Roshni and her friends are seen ministering to IDF girls, providing them with the hope and strength needed for the challenges ahead. The world has witnessed the devastating impact of terrorist actions on these precious lives, making their ministry all the more vital.

> *To bestow on them a crown of beauty instead of ashes, the oil of joy instead of mourning, and a garment of praise instead of a spirit of despair. They will be called oaks of righteousness, a planting of the Lord for the display of his splendour.* - Isaiah 61:3

With Joel, Roshni and Merlyn. *But as for me and my household, we will serve the Lord.* Joshua 24:15

FINDING YOUR SUNRISE

A Sunrise Wedding of Roshni and Joel.

> *"Let us rejoice and be glad and give him glory! For the wedding of the Lamb has come, and his bride has made herself ready."* — Revelation 19:7

> *"Fine linen, bright and clean, was given her to wear."* — Revelation 19:8
> (*Fine linen stands for the righteous acts of God's holy people.*)

A new beginning under the sunrise — a glimpse of eternity in every vow.

> *"The grace of our Lord Jesus Christ be with you all. Amen."* – Revelation 22:21

THE ETERNAL SUNRISE

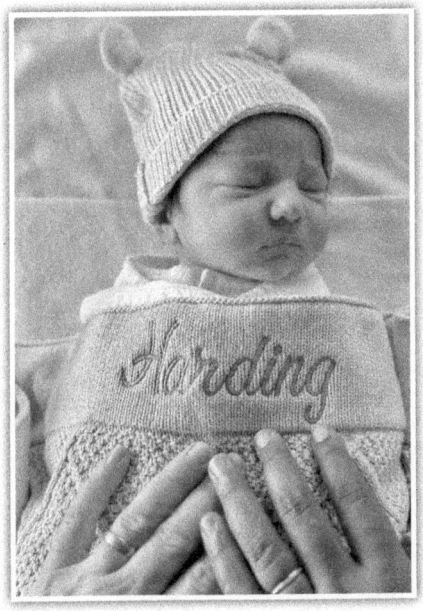

Our Grandson and our New Sunrise: **Solomon Ravi Harding**.

Roshni my daughter and Joel my son in law, chose the name Solomon because it means "peace". Our prayer is that Solomon will be a peacemaker—someone whose presence brings calm, wisdom, and light into the world.

I was then blessed to find out they had chosen my name Ravi, which means "sun" in Sanskrit —a symbol of light and life, as his middle name. I was filled with gratitude for God's goodness to know this child as "Sunrise Solomon".

The verse which inspired his name is Daniel 12:3:

> *"Those who are wise will shine as bright as the sky, and those who lead many to righteousness will shine like the stars forever."*

NOTES AND BIBLIOGRAPHY

1. Audio Teaching:
   Derek Prince Ministries. (n.d.). *Use and abuse of the tongue* [Audio file]. Derek Prince Ministries. Retrieved January 7, 2025, from:
   https://store-us.derekprince.com
2. Prince, D. (1993). *Does your tongue need healing?* Whitaker House.
3. Online Resource (Internet Archive):
   Prince, D. (1993). *Does your tongue need healing?* [eBook]. Whitaker House. Retrieved January 7, 2025, from:
   https://archive.org/details/doesyourtoguene0000prin
4. Derek Prince Ministries. (n.d.). *Use and abuse of the tongue - Part 1B* [Video]. YouTube. Retrieved January 15, 2025, from: https://www.youtube.com/watch?v=pwi_UmMcbSw
5. Dickey, E. J. (2000). *Liar's Game*. Dutton.
6. Lewis, C.S. *(1952)*. *Mere Christianity*. New York: HarperOne.
7. American Association of Neurological Surgeons (AANS). (n.d.). *Laminectomy*. Retrieved from https://www.aans.org/Patients/Neurosurgical-Conditions-and-Treatments/Laminectomy

8. National Institute of Neurological Disorders and Stroke (NINDS). (n.d.). *Arteriovenous Malformations (AVMs)*. Retrieved from https://www.ninds.nih.gov/
9. Jastrow, R. (n.d.). *God and the Astronomers*.
10. Phil Wickham's song "You're Beautiful" features the lyrics:
11. Goodrich, R. E. (2015). *Smile anyway: Quotes, verses, and grumblings for every day of the year.* CreateSpace Independent Publishing Platform.
12. Tagore, R. (1916). *Stray Birds.* The Macmillan Company.
13. Glosbe. (n.d.). راوی - *Persian-English Dictionary*. Retrieved from https://glosbe.com/fa/en/راوی
14. Monier-Williams, M. (1899). *A Sanskrit-English Dictionary.* Oxford University Press.
15. Law of *Karma,* Retrieved January 9, 2025, from https://philosophy.lander.edu/oriental/caste.html?utm_source=chatgpt.com
16. Eaton, R. (2005). *A Social History of the Deccan, 1300-1761: Eight Indian Lives.* Cambridge University Press.
17. Mishra, P. (2018). *From "Anna" to "Abba": 70 Indian Words Added to the Oxford Dictionary.* The Economic Times. Retrieved from economictimes.com
18. Gandhi, M. K. (1928). *An Autobiography: The Story of My Experiments with Truth.* Navajivan Publishing House.
19. "Basavanna Jayanti: The history, teachings and life story of Lord Basaveshwara." *The Art of Living India.* Art of Living, Retrieved December 1, 2024, from
20. ClearIAS. (n.d.). *Basavanna: Renowned Social Reformer.* Retrieved December 1, 2025, from https://www.clearias.com

21. "Basava." *Wikipedia*. Retrieved from: https://en.wikipedia.org/wiki/Basava?utm_source=chatgpt.com
22. "Caste System in India – Origin, Features, and Problems." *ClearIAS*. Retrieved December 1, 2024. from: https://divine-hindu.com/hinduism/reincarnation-in-hinduism-moksha-explained/
23. Mahadevan, S. *Scorpion Sting and Public Health*. Chennai Medical Publishing, 2001.
24. Jones, H. "Rural Venomous Encounters." *Journal of Tropical Medicine*, vol. 15, no. 3, 1998, pp. 67–82.
25. Indian Pediatrics. "Scorpion Sting Case Report." *Indian Pediatrics*, vol. 37, no. 5, 2000, pp. 504–514.
26. Warren, R. (2023). *Created to Dream: The 6 Phases God Uses to Grow Your Faith*. Zondervan.
27. Smith, L. H. (2014). *Seeing the Voice of God: What God Is Telling You Through Dreams and Visions*. Chosen Books.
28. Top 10 Books on Divine Storytelling and Spiritual Growth. (n.d.). *SoBrief*.
29. "Understanding the Meaning of Grace and Mercy." (2023). *Bible Study Tools*.
30. "What Does Romans 8:28 Mean?" (2022). *Ligonier Ministries*.
31. Prince, D., & Prince, R. (2008). *God Is a Matchmaker: Seven Biblical Principles for Finding Your Mate*. Chosen Books.
32. Evans, T. (n.d.). *The Godly Gift of Marriage*. Tony Evans Ministries.
33. "God Is the Ultimate Matchmaker." (2013). *The Bottom Line Ministries*.

34. Jones, R. (2018). Ancient migrations and genetic links between Australia's Indigenous peoples and South India. *Cultural Anthropology Review, 12*(3), 45-67.
35. The Deceitful Heart and the New Covenant" by David Guzik. *Enduring Word Bible Commentary.* https://enduringword.com/bible-commentary/jeremiah-17/?utm_source=chatgpt.com
36. Packer, J. I. (1973). *Knowing God.* InterVarsity Press.
37. "The Reality of the Sinful Nature" by Bible Hub Staff. *Bible Hub.*
38. Asato Ma Sadgamaya – In Sanskrit with Meaning." (n.d.). *Green* https://greenmesg.org/stotras/vedas/om_asato_ma_sadgamaya.php?utm_source
39. "The Transformative Power of Scripture." (n.d.). *Bible Hub.*
40. "The Importance of Personal Relationship with God." (n.d.). *Bible Hub.*
41. "10 Reasons To Believe In The Bible." (2023). *Bible Wisdom Hub.*
42. "Ephesians 2:8-9 Commentary." (n.d.). *Precept Austin.* https://www.preceptaustin.org/ephesians_28-9?utm_source
43. Reagan, D. (2017). *Israel in Bible Prophecy: Past, Present & Future.* Lamb & Lion Ministries.
44. "Israel: Still a Miracle." (2003). *Israel My Glory.*
45. TemplePurohit. "Symbolism and Significance of Vibhuti." *TemplePurohit,* 2019. Retrieved January 15, 2025, from https://www.templepurohit.com/symbolism-significance-vibhuti.
46. VedicTribe. "What is Vibhuti or Bhasma and its Significance in Hinduism?" *VedicTribe,* 2019. https://vedictribe.com/dharma/hinduism/what-is-vibhuti-or-bhasma-and-its-significance-in-hinduism/.

47. Painters Best. "Aboriginal Body Paint: The Origins of This Ancient Body Art." *Painters Best*, 2023. https://paintersbest.com/aboriginal-body-paint/.
48. Marradreaming. "The Significance of Ochre in Aboriginal Australian Art." *Marradreaming*, 2024.
49. The-significance-of-ochre-in-aboriginal-australian-art.An ancient Australian connection to India?
50. Retrieved January 15, 2025, from https://www.marradreaming.com.au/post/Ancient migration: Genes link Australia with India - BBC News Ancient migration: Genes link Australia with India - BBC News.
51. Basu, A., Sarkar-Roy, N., & Majumder, P. P. (2009). *Genomic reconstruction of the Indian-Australian phylogenetic link*. BMC Evolutionary Biology, 9(173). Retrieved January 15, 2025, from https://bmcecolevol.biomedcentral.com/articles/10.1186/1471-2148-9-173
52. George Washington

    "It is impossible to rightly govern a nation without God and the Bible." Reference: Writings of George Washington, Vol. 35 (John C. Fitzpatrick, Ed.).
53. Theodore Roosevelt

    "A thorough knowledge of the Bible is worth more than a college education." Reference: The Man in the Arena: Speeches and Essays (1920).

NOTES AND BIBLIOGRAPHY

54. Mahatma Gandhi
 "*You Christians look after a document containing enough dynamite to blow all civilisation to pieces, turn the world upside down, and bring peace to a battle-torn planet.*"
 Reference: E. Stanley Jones, "The Christ of the Indian Road" (1925).
55. Munroe, M. (n.d.). *The wealthiest place in the world is not the gold mines...* [Quote]. Goodreads. Retrieved November 1, 2024 from: https://www.goodreads.com/quotes/9196732-the-wealthiest-place-in-the-world-is-not-the-gold
56. Quirós's Proclamation: Renewal Journal
57. Historical Context: Partners in Prayer and Evangelism - Australia's Destiny
58. General Background: Sandhurst Diocese - How Australia Got Its European Name
59. Hindmarsh, B. A. (2001). *John Newton and the English Evangelical Tradition: Between the Conversions of Wesley and Wilberforce.* Oxford University Press.
60. International Institute for Creation Research. "Scientific Case Against Evolution." Accessed January 27, 2025. https://www.icr.org/home/resources/resources_tracts_scientificcaseagainstevolution
61. Discovery Institute. "Irreducible Complexity: The Challenge to Darwinian Evolution." Accessed January 27, 2025. https://www.discovery.org/a/24041
62. Carrington, Damian. "Do We Need a New Theory of Evolution?" *The Guardian*, June 28, 2022. Accessed January

27, 2025. https://www.theguardian.com/science/2022/jun/28/do-we-need-a-new-theory-of-evolution
63. Federal Aviation Administration (FAA). *(2021). Pitot Tube Blockage and Its Impact on Flight Safety.* FAA Safety Briefing. Retrieved from www.faa.gov
64. James, M. (2018). *Aircraft Pitot-Static System Contamination and the Role of Insect Nests.* Aerospace Safety Journal, 45(3), 112-118.
65. Federal Aviation Administration (FAA). *(2021). Aircraft Structural Integrity and Corrosion Prevention.* FAA Advisory Circular AC 43-4B. Retrieved from www.faa.gov
66. National Transportation Safety Board (NTSB). *(2020). Aircraft Structural Failures: Causes, Prevention, and Safety Measures.* Washington, DC: NTSB Reports.
67. Coleman, Robert E. – *The Master Plan of Evangelism* (1963)
68. Stanley, Andy, and Lane Jones – *Communicating for a Change: Connecting with the People Your Faith Matters Most to* (2007)
69. Fee, Gordon D. and Stuart, Douglas – *How to Read the Bible for All Its Worth* (2003)
70. Raj, Peniel. *(2002). Robert de Nobili and the Adaptation of Christianity in India.* Delhi: ISPCK.

NOTES AND BIBLIOGRAPHY

Additional Resources

Munroe, M. (1992). *Understanding Your Potential: Discovering the Hidden You.* Whitaker House.
This book contains his extensive teachings on potential and its connection to purpose.

The Narratologist Compilation

Best Myles Munroe Quotes on Purpose. (n.d.). The Narratologist. Retrieved December 1, 2024, from: https://www.thenarratologist.com/best-myles-munroe-quotes-on-purpose/

Interview/Media Reference

Munroe often shared this message in his public seminars and interviews. An example includes his sermon on potential available on platforms like YouTube under titles like *"The Tragedy of the Cemetery."*

Dr. Myles Munroe, a renowned motivational speaker and author, often emphasised the concept of untapped potential and the tragedy of unfulfilled dreams. He famously stated, "The wealthiest place in the world is not the gold mines of South America or the oil fields of Iraq or Iran. They are not the diamond mines of South Africa or the banks of the world. The wealthiest place on the planet is just down the road. It is the cemetery. There lie buried companies that were never started, inventions that were never made, bestselling books that were never written, and masterpieces that were never painted. In the cemetery is buried the greatest treasure of untapped potential.

Sharing Your Faith With a Hindu by Madasamy Thirumalai
 This book provides practical insights into Hindu beliefs and how to communicate the Gospel respectfully within their cultural framework.

The Jesus Way to India's Heart by M. Ezra Sargunam
 A resourceful guide on evangelism in India, highlighting ways to build meaningful relationships while sharing Christ's love.

Finding Your Hindu Ancestors in Christ by Vishal Mangalwadi
 Vishal Mangalwadi explores the parallels between Hindu traditions and biblical truths, offering tools for contextualising the Gospel.

Christ-Centered Sharing of the Gospel to Hindus by Bob Blincoe
 This book focuses on culturally sensitive approaches to introducing Jesus to Hindus.

Hinduism: A Christian Introduction by Peter Cotterell
 An in-depth exploration of Hinduism from a Christian perspective, equipping believers with the knowledge to engage in meaningful dialogue.

The Unexpected Adventure: Taking Everyday Risks to Talk with People about Jesus by Lee Strobel and Mark Mittelberg
 Though not India-specific, this book offers universal principles for sharing the Gospel, including relatable anecdotes applicable in the Indian context.

NOTES AND BIBLIOGRAPHY

Cultural Keys to Unlocking the Gospel for South Asians by Nathan George
A guide for understanding the cultural nuances of South Asian communities and sharing the Gospel in ways that resonate with their worldview.

Engaging with Hindus: Understanding Their World; Sharing Good News by Robin Thomson
A concise and practical handbook for engaging with Hindu neighbours, understanding their worldview, and sharing the hope of the Gospel.

Derek Prince Ministries has made significant efforts to reach and equip Indian Christians through the translation and distribution of Derek Prince's teachings. One notable compilation is "Life-Changing Spiritual Power," which includes six of Derek Prince's books:

- "*The Divine Exchange*"
- "*How to Pass from Curse to Blessing*"
- "*The Holy Spirit in You*"

www.ingramcontent.com/pod-product-compliance
Lightning Source LLC
Chambersburg PA
CBHW032109090426
42743CB00007B/294